PUFFIN BC

Editor : Kaye

SUMMER WITH TOMMY

Thirty pounds was what he cost – a tiny bay cross-bred wild pony, only 11.2 hands high. Curious, intelligent and lively, Tommy made his summer with Caroline Silver a summer to remember. He fell ill, and was nursed back to health by Caroline. And his dependence upon her while he was ill forged a bond between them that made training him easy. He would follow her anywhere, his nose in the small of her back, more like a large dog than a pony. He also developed other, less endearing, habits: he could escape through the most horse-proof of fences; he walked freely into other people's kitchens; he trampled through the neighbouring farmers' fields, and made the most deplorable horse friends.

But he learned lungeing, long-reining, to carry a rider, the rein-back, the forehand turn, leading off on either leg at a canter, jumping, and to go freely, mounted, across country. He became perfect in traffic and, in fact, turned into the ideal children's pony, with a lively and lovable character. In six months he had changed from a shy, ignorant little animal into a confident and reliable friend.

Summer with Tommy is a touching and funny story and also a careful instruction book for any young rider to follow.

CAROLINE SILVER

Summer with Tommy

Training a Wild Pony

with photographs by
PATRICK THURSTON,
BYRON TRAVERS, NATHAN SILVER
and RODDY MAUDE-ROXBY

PUFFIN BOOKS

Puffin Books, Penguin Books Ltd, Harmondsworth, Middlesex, England
Penguin Books Australia Ltd, Ringwood, Victoria, Australia
Penguin Books Canada Ltd, 41 Steelcase Road West, Markham, Ontario, Canada
Penguin Books (N.Z.) Ltd, 182–190 Wairau Road, Auckland 10, New Zealand

—

First published by Jonathan Cape 1974
Published in Puffin Books 1976
Copyright © Caroline Silver 1974

—

Made and printed in Great Britain by
Butler & Tanner Ltd, Frome and London
Set in 12/14 pt Meridien

Thanks are due to the *Daily Telegraph*
Colour Library for permission
to reproduce the photographs by
Patrick Thurston included in this book

If oxen and horses or lions had hands, and could paint with their hands, and produce works of art as men do, horses would paint the forms of gods like horses.

— XENOPHANES

CONTENTS

8   *Contents*

Chapter 1

CAN'T GET MUCH FOR £30

I work as a writer. It is a job that I like, but what I like better than anything is being with horses and ponies. So, whenever possible, I try to get a commission to write about them.

I wanted to have a pony again, so I said to the *Daily Telegraph Magazine*, what about an article on training a wild pony? It would mean, I told them, that I would have to buy a wild pony and break it in, so that we could get a true story and take photographs to illustrate it. They very nicely said, 'All right, that sounds like a good idea. We'll give you £30 to get a pony, and you can write about it.' So I did; and I had such an interesting time that I thought I would write a book as well.

And that is how I came to buy Tommy. But before I bought him I had to make up my mind what I wanted – I thought it important to decide what I wanted before I started looking, so that I didn't get distracted by charming ponies who were unsuitable – and I had to do some research into the sort of pony I could buy for £30. It was a long time since I had bought a pony and, though the cost of ponies goes up all the time, fashions in breeds and colours change. Unfashionable breeding and colour means you get more pony for the price.

I looked through the advertisements in *Horse and Hound*. These, even if they don't include the pony you're looking for, give a very fair idea of demand and supply and of the type of pony that is currently popular. Prices, often, are on the hopeful side. So, sometimes, is the wording of the ads. 'Has seen hounds' will commend a young horse (but what is this fleeting glimpse worth?); another will say 'genuine reason for sale' (perhaps the pony is a lunatic); or 'warranted sound in wind, limb, and action' (but they don't say it isn't blind). Some of the advertisements I read said that the horse advertised had a vet's certificate of sound-ness, and I remembered a horse-dealer friend in South Wales who wanted to sell a mare who had something wrong with her hip. He had five vets to look at her before he found one who didn't notice the unsoundness and signed the certificate.

The last time I bought a pony, which was when I was eight, the fashionable colour was bay – preferably dark. Chestnut and grey ponies were then thought just about O.K., though a bit flashy, and coloured ponies were absolutely out. Now I found that the fashion went with cream and palomino ponies, and that the highest-priced was the spotted Appaloosa, which sold at basic pony price plus about £5 per spot. The cheapest pony colour, when I went to look for Tommy, was bay.

In 1948 you could buy a wild pony off the Welsh moors for 12s. 6d. ($62\frac{1}{2}$p) – not a very good pony, certainly: decent unbroken ponies went for about £3–£5. Since then, demand from foreign buyers, mainly German and Belgian, has brought prices of the best pure-bred ponies up to nearly four figures. The growing popularity of pony-riding in the British Isles has, of course, increased the cost of ponies of all kinds.

I found that anything that might have a chance in the show ring, or anything that could be bred from, would cost much more than £30, no matter how wild it was. And any of the lovely native breeds – Welsh, Dartmoor, Exmoor – anything that had a pedigree, even a half-breed, could be ruled out because of the price. All the really cheap ponies were mixtures.

At first I considered buying from one of the moorland pony fairs, which are great fun to go to, or from Stow Fair in Gloucestershire, where rejects from the moorland fairs are re-offered and all manner of local cross-breeds can be found. Dealers' prices at such fairs are reasonable, since rather than bid against each other they will often agree among themselves who will purchase what. But a couple of telephone calls to horse-transport agencies established that, unfortunately, the saving on the price of the pony would be cancelled out by the high cost of shipping it home to Cambridge.

There remained word of mouth from friends, which is often useful if you want a 'made' pony that someone has grown out of, but is pretty useless if you are looking for an unbroken pony; and dealers. I am naturally suspicious about horse-dealers (though I have never had cause to be), and my distrust was made worse by the local vet. 'I wouldn't back most veterinary surgeons against a horse-dealer,' he told me. 'Not if the dealer's got something to cover up. Covering up is the horse-dealer's speciality, and he's damn good at it.'

He also told me that most vets know very little about horses. 'It's almost impossible to know everything about all animals,' he explained. 'Especially now that the most valuable animal is getting to be the chicken.' He said that only about one vet in six is capable of giving an opinion on a horse, and that if I wanted to be sure I was getting the best advice I should consult a vet who was a member of the British Equine Association.

Since asking a veterinary surgeon to give his opinion on a pony must cost a bit for his time and travelling, I ruled out the experts and decided to trust to luck. I knew what I wanted – a small, unbroken mongrel, at least three years old so that he would be strong enough to be broken in. (It's all very well for racehorses to be broken in at eighteen months, but they get special food from birth. Ponies don't.) I knew that he would have to be purchased locally if I wanted to spend the money on the pony and not on the shipping. And I knew – since advertisements in horsey magazines hadn't offered what I was looking for – that I would have to go to a dealer.

With some misgiving, and at the recommendation of a friend, I called up a dealer in ponies and donkeys with the curious name of A. Bray. Had he, I asked, got a cheap, un-broken three-year-old, Welsh-type, for not more than £30? As it happened, Mr Bray said, he had just the thing: a dark bay gelding, halter-broken, not pretty. The price he wanted for it was, coincidentally, £30.

As it happened, I needn't have worried. If I am ever lucky enough to have another pony I'll ask Mr Bray to get it for me, because he sold me a marvellous pony at a fair price. He sold me Tommy.

Chapter 2

A SCRUFFY LITTLE OBJECT

It was almost the end of April when I went to see A. Bray. The bluebells, which were late because of the cold, had only just started to open and I still hadn't heard a cuckoo. Mr Bray lived with an assortment of livestock on a farm about twelve miles from me. Geese, ducks, and dogs hooted and quacked and barked as I drove into the yard. Ponies and donkeys grazed in the paddocks, or peered at me over the doors of innumerable sheds and barns.

Mr Bray was an extraordinary figure – very tall, quite young, with hardly any teeth and one eye half-closed as though in a permanent wink. He wore a cowman's smock over his shirt and trousers, a light brown article that stopped just short of his knees. My doubts about horse-dealers got stronger at the sight of him; and at the sound of him – nearly every sentence began with, 'To be perfectly truthful' or, 'To be honest with you' – got worse. He showed me around the yard; showed me twenty or more ponies, whose prices I forebore to ask, though they were sometimes volunteered. I enjoyed it, but I was waiting to see what I had come for: the small, dark bay, three-year-old gelding, un-broken and unpretty, who I hoped would be suitable to buy.

After a while Mr Bray got fed up with showing me his other animals, probably because I didn't look like buying any of them, and called to his boy to bring the youngster out of the barn. I asked if I could see the pony before he was brought out. Mr Bray assented, and thus I had my first sight of Tommy – a scruffy-looking little object, very tiny, with a thick, dull coat, wearing a halter much too big for him and tied to a post in a barn full of other ponies. He shrank away as we came closer, moving off as far as the rope would let him and looking at us with interested, rather nervous, brown eyes. I agreed with Mr Bray: he wasn't what anyone would call pretty. He was, however, narrow, which I think is a good thing in a child's pony, and I couldn't see much wrong with his conformation except, perhaps, that his head was a bit on the big side. He had a very real curiosity about us, which suggested to me that he was probably intelligent. He wouldn't let me examine him too closely, but shied away round the other side of the post, watching me all the time.

Mr Bray's boy untied the rope and led Tommy outside. He walked the pony away from me; then he walked him towards me. Then he walked him past, sideways on. The pony walked beautifully, with a nice clean action. Mr Bray's boy took the pony out into the lane and went through the same procedure at a trot. I was surprised and delighted – Tommy carried himself really well, arching his thin neck and pointing his toes like a miniature show hack. He had, for such a midget, a long, free, elastic trot. 'Nice mover,' said Mr Bray, unnecessarily.

When they brought him back into the barn, Tommy let me – he hadn't any choice with three adult humans round him – run a hand over his body to feel for bumps or scars or heat. There weren't any. I had a look in his mouth to see if there were any missing teeth, poked a finger near to each eye to see if he blinked (he did: if he hadn't, it would have meant blindness or very bad sight), ran a hand down his legs to see that they were smooth and firm and cool, and picked up his feet, which were excellent – round and neat, with no cracks in the wall of the hoof. Tommy's furry coat was rough to my touch, and he shivered away from my unfamiliar hand. I felt pretty sure it was from genuine wildness, since his eyes hadn't the hopeless look of a pony who shies away from the touch because it expects rough treatment.

'Has this pony been running wild from birth?' I asked Mr Bray, rather surprised that a pony could grow to three years old nowadays without being used to the touch of humans. 'No idea,' he said. 'I bought him from a dealer in Cheshire, along with a truckload of other ponies. He's only been here a day or two.' And that was all I was ever to learn about the past life of Tommy.

I stayed and chatted to Mr Bray for a bit longer, interested in some of the things he told me about pony-buyers. 'Most people who come into my yard fancy just one pony from the start, and almost always end up buying it,' he said.

'Is it usually the best pony?' I asked.

'Hardly ever.'

'Then why do you concern yourself about it?'

'Because the moment I spot it, that pony ends up costing them an extra twenty quid,' he replied, with endearing honesty.

I asked if I could have an option on Tommy until the following morning, because I wanted to think it over by my-self. This was readily given, and we arranged that if I bought the pony he would drop it off from his truck when he was next passing through Cambridge. Then I said goodbye and thank you to Mr Bray, who winked at me – or didn't; I still couldn't make up my mind about his eye – and drove off home.

I thought about Tommy all the way home, and well into the night. I decided he had great potential. Probably he would make a nice ride, if his trot was anything to go by, and the intelligent and kindly look about him suggested that he would make an amusing and affectionate little animal for someone to have fun with.

I felt the same when I woke up next day, so I called up Mr Bray and offered him £30 for the pony if he would deliver it to my door the next time he came through Cambridge. He said he wasn't coming through Cambridge in the near future, and that he wouldn't hang on to the pony until then, 'because if I keep him hanging about here he'll have eaten a couple of quid's worth of grub by the time he leaves, and then where's my profit?' This seemed reasonable enough, so we settled for £31 if Tommy was delivered to me the next afternoon. Mr Bray said it would cost him a pound a mile to make the special journey in his truck, but we both knew that he was exaggerating.

The next afternoon passed slowly. I was, I found, very excited about the pony, and spent most of the time in the drive waiting for the truck to arrive. When, by four o'clock, nothing had happened, I couldn't wait any longer and called Mr Bray to see if anything was the matter. He answered the telephone himself. 'To be perfectly truthful,' he said, 'I was just picking up the phone to call you. Only I didn't have your number.

'My bloomin' truck's not back yet, madam,' he explained. 'I'll deliver it in the morning, provided nothing happens to my truck.'

Something happened to Mr Bray's truck the next morning. To be honest with me, it broke down and he didn't really want to drive it anywhere until he could be sure it wouldn't break down again. He would try to deliver the pony that afternoon.

I waited through the early part of the afternoon, still excited about the idea of having a pony but resigned to not having it that day; and surprisingly, at about three o'clock the truck rolled up, driven by Mr Bray. I had made arrangements for the pony to be pastured in a paddock a mile and a half from my home – the nearest I could get in built-up Cambridge, since I had no grazing of my own. Though there were fields much nearer to where I lived, there were other ponies in them and I wanted to put Tommy in a paddock by himself so that he would have to depend on me for his social life. Mr Bray offered to drive us over.

When we got there I hopped out of the box to make sure that everything was ready. The paddock, about two acres, was rich in new spring grass, which was probably not yet as nourishing as it looked, and there were trees for shade and for shelter in bad weather. I had inspected the fences the day before, had gone over the grass looking for bits of wire or tin that could hurt the pony and had cleaned out and filled the water trough, so there wasn't much to check. Then Mr Bray let down the side of his enormous cattle truck and led out my very small pony. We said goodbye, and he climbed back into his cab and started up the engine.

I led Tommy to his new home. Before letting him loose, I stayed and chatted to him for a while, giving him carrots and apples and sugar lumps so that he would know I was a friend. I decided to leave the headcollar on him because he might be difficult to catch, and when I eventually unclipped the lead-rope he was so happy to be free that he gave a couple of wild bucks and raced away across his new land. Then he rolled.

I left him to get on with it, and walked back to the road. To my surprise, a cattle truck was parked on the pavement a couple of hundred yards away. Mr Bray's boots stuck out from under the engine. His truck had broken down again.

Chapter 3

CATCH AS CATCH CAN

Anyone who has tried to catch a wild pony in a space too big for it to be cornered will guess how I spent the next few days. Luckily, I had an idea that it would be difficult, and remembered to take a book with me to the paddock, along with oats, grooming kit, and a lead-rope. On the first afternoon I thought I might as well at least *try* to go up to Tommy, so I put some oats in a shallow bowl where he could see them and walked towards him, holding out the food and talking gently. He stood his ground until I was about ten yards away, stiff and apprehensive but curious about the food; then he wheeled and galloped off to the far side of the field, where he turned and snorted at me. Oh, all right, I thought, seeing that pursuit would be futile and would only excite him more. I put the bowl of oats down in the grass where Tommy could see it, and lay down near them, glad that it was a fine day. Since I expected to be there for some time, I opened the book.

Tommy took his time about it. At first he ran round the field, bucking and snorting and making it quite clear that if I thought I could catch him I must be out of my head. At the end of each gallop he stopped short and turned to face me, blowing the air down his nose in great snorts of nervous outrage. After a while he settled down and began to graze, staying well over on the far side of the paddock and keeping an eye on me all the time. An hour or two passed. It was warm in the sun, and the grass smelled rich and sweet. A grasshopper landed on my book, cleaned its legs in the sun for a bit, and took off when I turned the page. From the stronghold of an evil master-mind, high up in the Swiss Alps, James Bond made a spectacular escape on skis; and when I looked up, Tommy, still grazing, was closer to me.

I got to the end of the book and sat up. It was nearly six o'clock: I had been there four hours, and was stiff. Tommy, who was quite near, drew back a pace or two and snorted at me. I reached out slowly for the oats and shook them, hoping he would be able to smell them, but he changed his mind and trotted away to the end of the paddock. Within a quarter of an hour he was back, circling round me with stiff, delicate steps and looking hungrily at the oats. I spoke to him all the time, trying to sound calm and quiet although I was secretly elated to have him come so close of his own accord. He came as near as he dared, his neck stretched out for the food, and finally, with great boldness, took the last brave step and knocked the bowl over. This shook him into a retreat; but this time he pulled up only thirty yards away and came back quite quickly, spurred on by an obvious longing for the oats. He grabbed a mouthful and threw his head up, tense all over. The shy brown eyes never left me for an instant – but the jaw was working.

It was fairly easy after that. Tommy's head went down into the spilled oats and he ate ravenously, watching me all the time. I didn't try to catch him, but sat watching and talking to him, and when he had finished and had eaten some of the grass where the oats had been I reached slowly into my jeans pocket and offered him an apple, cut into quarters to make it easier for him to eat. The whiskery little muzzle tickled against my fingers, the stretched-out mouth grabbed the bits of apple, and Tommy was off two yards from me. He stretched out his nose again and sniffed at me; then, apparently deciding that I had no more to offer, settled to graze.

It was late, and I had dinner to cook. I went away very slowly on all fours, trying not to make any sudden movement, and Tommy did not take fright at this odd human exit but only raised his head and watched me go.

Next day the water trough needed topping up, so I did that before making any advances to Tommy. He came quite close while I worked, curious to see what was going on, but galloped off when I held out the oats to him. I sat down in the grass and opened my book, keeping the bowl of oats within reach; he was genuinely frightened of me, but if he was ever to learn that I was a friend then the sooner he was caught and reassured the better. The catching took just under three hours: he galloped about, snorting; grazed, pretending to pay no attention to me; came close and blew at me suspiciously; finally he got his nose into the oats, and my hand, which had been resting on the edge of the bowl, moved slowly up and closed on his headcollar. The next part of the operation was worrying because I needed to get up on my feet to be able to hold him firmly, yet any sudden movement would be sure to frighten him; and if he got loose again now, I thought, I'd be there all week before he let me get hold of him again.

I got up slowly, and the pony shot backwards and almost pulled me off my feet. I fastened the lead-rope on to the headcollar and offered him some oats by hand, and by degrees he calmed down and let me lead him to the fence, where I tied him up and put the oats down by his head. Provided that I made no abrupt movement, Tommy didn't seem to mind having a brush run over his shaggy coat. His mane was a mess – it stood up like a bush – his long, straggling tail was matted, and his thick winter coat came out under the brush in chunks. He was apparently unused to having his feet handled, making it more difficult when I tried to pick them up by leaning his weight on the leg I wanted, so that I had to push into his body to get him to lean away. Then his head came up, and so did his near fore, and I held it briefly and praised him for his good behaviour.

When the oats were finished, we went for a walk. I led him around the paddock for a minute or two, and when I was sure that he was obedient and quite accustomed to being led and that I could control him (my comparative size helped, as it was to do all through his breaking in) we went out into the road for a walk. It was a quiet side road with a grass verge, and on this we went for a mile or two, occasionally breaking into a trot. Tommy showed signs of interest, pricking his ears and looking about him, and I hoped he would think work fun and would associate this pleasant exercise with me. I had him back at the paddock in about half an hour, before he had a chance to get bored, and gave him some praise and some carrots before turning him loose.

That was how it went all week. After three or four days, though the initial snorting and galloping about went on as usual and the shyness was still very much in evidence, the time between settling down to graze and allowing himself to be caught had shortened to less than an hour. A private

road ran along one side of the paddock, and passers-by often stopped to look at Tommy, which must have helped him to get used to people.

The weather was curious for the time of year: on the second morning after Tommy arrived I woke up to find snow on the ground, but by late in the day it had usually turned to warm spring weather. In the scented evenings of early May we walked together round the back roads of Cambridge, or went off along footpaths across the fields. Every so often we would meet a car, and I would wave to it to slow down and would put my arm around Tommy's neck, standing between him and the noisy monster while he shivered all over with fright. Most of the drivers were kind, stopping when they saw my signal, but a few, who were perhaps not used to ponies and thought a horse on the road must presumably know about traffic, came by too fast and too close and frightened Tommy badly.

On one of these evenings we went to my home, where the unfamiliar sound of hooves on the gravel brought out Magnificat, the cat, and her two kittens who were eight weeks old. Magnificat, or Nif as she is usually called, is an Abyssinian, the sculptured sort of cat that the ancient Egyptians used to worship. She has dense, short fur the colour of a wild hare, and like all Abyssinians she is affectionate, intelligent, curious and brave. The kittens, also purebred Abyssinians, were easily as bold and as inquisitive as their mother, and when Tommy and I went round the side of the house and on to the back lawn the whole cat family came after us for a closer look, Nif leading the way.

Nif had never seen a pony before and was most intrigued, though rather shy when Tommy wanted to smell her. The kittens, on the other hand, had no inhibitions (at one point they even tried to climb up Tommy's leg), so they had to be picked up and carried indoors out of harm's way.

On the evening of May 3rd, when I had had Tommy for five days, we went for a long walk across the fields to Grantchester. There were a few busy roads to negotiate before we crossed the common and got on to the Grantchester footpath. It was a path meant for people only, with little gates intended to keep animals out, but Tommy – no wider than a fat adult – could squeeze through most of them quite easily. When we were nearly at the village we were stopped by an impossibly small gate (I wondered how the fat people of Grantchester managed: perhaps there aren't any?) and forced to turn back. The way home led through a water meadow, with little drainage ditches thickly overgrown with wild iris, offering a natural opportunity to see if Tommy could jump. Meaning to set him an example, I went over the ditches first, and got bogged down in the mud on the other side. Tommy jumped much better than I did: with no hesitation at all he gathered himself together and sprang, jumping well clear of the mud in big leaps with his front feet pointed neatly together on landing. He seemed to enjoy it, and after the first two or three ditches was jumping alongside rather than behind me. I stopped him after half a dozen ditches, because I did not want him to get bored, and let him pick a bit of the rich new grass as a reward. The trees on the edge of the meadow were beginning to fill out with green, and in a hawthorn bush on the side of the path a blackbird sang.

For the past two days, as Tommy became increasingly easy in my company, I had been leaning against him whenever we stopped for a bit of grass, and had several times put my full weight across his back and fractionally lifted my toes off the ground. It was, properly speaking, much too early in our relationship for me to try backing him, but he had, it seemed, not minded my weight; so now, because he had been so good and quiet on our walk and perhaps a bit because the evening was so lovely, I slipped a leg over his back as he grazed and sat on him properly for the first time. It was a risky thing to do without an assistant to hold his head, because to a wild pony having something on its back is the most frightening thing there is. In the natural state it only happens when a predator, such as a mountain lion, drops from a tree or a cliff to kill it, and any pony's instinctive response to being backed for the first time must be to run and buck until it gets the killer off.

Tommy, however, paid no attention to me whatsoever; didn't even tense up his muscles. It was a strange feeling, sitting on his furry back – I had never been on so small a pony – and my feet hung down well below his knees. Had Tommy, I wondered, watching the calm little head grazing below me, already been backed? I got off after a minute in case he hadn't.

On the way home we tried it three times more. Tommy, at my suggestion, stopped to graze; I got on very carefully and sat on his back for a minute or two telling him how good he was, then slipped off and led him on. It didn't worry him in the least, and I began to wonder whether he had been not only backed, but ridden.

He hadn't, as I found out three days later when Prue Leith, a friend who is good with ponies, came down from London for the weekend to help with Tommy. The weather had turned wet and cold, and once or twice I had heard Tommy cough. We drove down to the field together, caught him fairly easily, tied him up and groomed him. I had brought along a clothes line, cut into two pieces, because I planned to give him his first lesson on the lunge. Lungeing, driving a pony in circles to the left or right, teaches balance and obedience, and I needed Prue's help because Tommy would not have the faintest idea what he was expected to do unless there was someone there at the start to lead him: to get him to go forward when I said 'Walk on', trot him at the command 'Trot', go back to 'Walk' when asked, and stop at 'Whoa'. I tied the clothes line to Tommy's head-collar – I couldn't afford a lunge rein, or the cavesson headcollar with the fixed, padded noseband that is the proper equipment for lungeing, and I don't think it really matters what the pony wears as long as he learns his lessons – and backed away about five yards. 'Walk on,' I said, moving a long piece of stick that was doing duty as a lunge whip up in the direction of Tommy's shaggy behind; and Prue, who had hold of the headcollar on the side nearest to me, started to lead the pony round. After a couple of circuits we tried going from a walk to a trot, and then back again to a walk and a halt, Prue's directions always synchronized with my words of command.

It was rather a failure. Tommy did as Prue told him, but only broke into a trot when she pulled quite hard on the headcollar. He was more unco-operative than I had yet seen him, and seemed uninterested in the lesson and a bit listless, so after ten minutes we decided to pack it in.

I had backed Tommy two or three times a day since the evening when we went to Grantchester, once or twice when he was tied up in his field. I would start by just leaning across his back, then carefully slide a leg over him and sit on his back for a minute or two.

Tommy had taken it calmly each time. Now, having Prue to help seemed too good an opportunity to pass up, so I got on his back again, and, asking her to lead him forward, said, 'Walk on.' Tommy took a couple of calm steps forward in

response to the pull on his halter, then his personality seemed to change: frightened at the feel of me on his back when moving (I suppose when I had backed him before he must have accepted it as a sort of leaning against him) he gave four great panic-stricken leaps. On the fourth buck I fell off, foolishly stretched my hand down to break the fall, and sprained my thumb. Once he had got rid of me, Tommy quietened down, and I was glad to see that Prue had managed to keep hold of him because our chances of catching him after a nasty experience like that would have been slight. Both of us talked to him and patted him until he was relaxed and confident, and then I slipped gently on to his back once more because I did not want to turn him loose without reasserting that the backing stage at least was all right. However, this time we made no attempt to move him.

After a minute or two, we thought he had had enough – we had, anyway, because the rain was starting to come down again and the afternoon, though warmer, was getting miserable. We tied him up and gave him some oats while we ran a brush over his dampening coat, more from ceremony than to get him clean, and suddenly Tommy's small frame went rigid and he started to cough. It came in bursts as we worked over his coat, and it bore in on me gradually that he was not much interested in his oats. One of his nostrils was running. I realized then, though far too late, that the listless behaviour on the lunge had been caused because Tommy was ill, and I felt monstrous about having asked him to work when he wasn't well. I should have known it, from the comparative ease we had in catching him, from the sluggish way he moved on the lunge, from the lack of interest in his feed. But I had missed all these signs, had backed him twice, and had asked him to accept a stranger when he could not have been feeling sociable.

We decided to take him in. We couldn't, we agreed, leave him out in what promised to be a night of heavy rain, and, though I had no stable, the toolshed should be big enough to house him and at least would keep him dry. Prue went ahead in the car to start on the heavy job of getting the tools outside, and I led Tommy slowly home. It felt like the longest journey I had ever made: we covered the one-and-a-half miles in just under two hours, with Tommy coughing very badly and dragging behind on his halter-rope. The gay little pony I had taken out for exercise all week no longer existed, and I wished, many times as the rain came solidly down, that I had a horsebox to take him back in or was strong enough to carry him home.

After what seemed a very long time indeed, we turned into the drive at home. Prue had cleared out the tools from the shed (a great heap of them stood stacked outside in the wet) and was carrying in armfuls of grass, which she had cut with shears from the bank in the back garden. I led Tommy into the toolshed, now knee-high in fresh-cut grass, and got him a bucket of water. We hadn't any straw to rub him down with, so we fetched a pile of towels from the airing cupboard and dried him off with those. Then I called the veterinary surgeon, who was, his secretary said, not available until Tuesday (this was Saturday) and anyway, she said, they were out of cough medicine. Tommy's coughs echoed from the grass-damp toolshed, and I frantically called the Cambridge School of Veterinary Medicine. Yes, they said, I could have some cough medicine to be going on with.

So Prue and I got out the car and drove over to fetch the cough medicine. The corn merchant, from whom I had hoped to get straw and hay, was closed for the weekend, and Tommy had to make do with our drying-out grass and the cough medicine, which we fed to him sandwiched in hunks of bread to disguise the taste. We left him, draught-free, clean-bedded, and not too damp, as the night closed in.

Because of this illness, which was to last for nearly a fortnight, Tommy learned to trust me and to count on me for everything that mattered. He didn't learn because he wanted to, but because he had no choice; and I suppose if I had a pony to train over again, and had the use of a stable, I would isolate him, whether ill or not, and make him dependent on me because it is the easiest way to break him in. But I wish I could have learned that without the price of Tommy having to be so ill.

Chapter 4

A WILD THING SORRY FOR ITSELF

On Sunday morning I went out to the toolshed before breakfast for a look at Tommy. He was lying down when I opened the door, but lurched to his feet at the sight of me and began to cough. It was a horrible sound, hard and dry. Tommy's eyes had a flat, hopeless look and his coat, which, though scruffy, had looked quite healthy when I bought him the week before, was dull and staring. Prue joined me after a moment, and the anxious look on her face said that she didn't like what she saw any more than I did.

He had finished up his water in the night, and thirstily drained the bucket when I fetched him some more. We gave him oats for breakfast, which was all we had, and threw in a few chopped-up apples and carrots to make the feed more interesting, but he hardly touched it. Nor was he interested in the armful of fresh grass we cut for him. Since he obviously needed to take his cough medicine and there didn't seem much chance that he would wolf it down in a piece of bread, I scooped some of the revolting sticky brown paste out of the pot, opened his unwilling mouth, and cleaned my fingers on the back of his tongue. He didn't like it much (nor did I) but he had to swallow it because it was too far back in his mouth for him to spit it out. Tommy

swallowed with such obvious discomfort that I thought
there might be something wrong with his throat, but an
examination showed nothing that I could spot – there were
no swollen glands or sensitive places, and the discharge
from his nose was very moderate. All the same we went
indoors to telephone for another vet because the pony was,
we decided, much too ill to wait until Tuesday before he got
medical attention. No one could come out to us that day,
but one very overworked man, hearing the desperation in
my voice, promised to come the following day.

After breakfast, Prue and I took the car out on a hunt
for straw, hay and oats, stopping at local farms until the car
was piled with the odds and ends we wanted. We came
home and cleaned out Tommy's grass bed, replacing it with
a deep, warm bed of straw. The pony's head hung listlessly,
indifferent to us and to our strange behaviour. Later in the
day, he did not even bother to get up when I came into the
toolshed, but let me offer him water (yes) and food (no)
while he was lying down.

The next morning he was just as bad, or worse. He hardly
touched his food, pushing it out of the way with his
lips or just letting his muzzle rest in the bowl. He didn't
drink much either, and the hay I had left for him the night
before had gone uneaten. He did not bother to get to his
feet, so I had to muck out round him and leave the bit of
bed he was lying on untouched. When I had finished, I sat
down with him in the clean straw and held his tired little
head in my hands, scratching the upper part of his face and
gently pulling his ears. He seemed to like this bit of fuss,
and leaned his head into my body so that his eyes were
hidden in my riding jacket.

It wasn't until late in the evening that the veterinary

surgeon arrived, looking tired and irritated and suggesting
by his manner that people who molly-coddled ponies were
fools. His attitude changed when he saw Tommy, and he
opened his bag and took the pony's temperature at once.
He looked at the thermometer, which registered a couple of
degrees above normal, and told me that Tommy had a cold.
This is a much more serious disease in ponies than in
humans because ponies have such a comparatively long
breathing apparatus. 'Where did you get him from?' asked
the vet, hoping to establish what diseases Tommy might
have been in contact with. I replied that as far as I knew
he had been through at least two dealers' hands recently.
'Then God knows what he's incubating,' he said, breaking open two large capsules and injecting the contents
into Tommy's neck. I asked what the injections were, and
the vet told me, in a short way that suggested he didn't
think it would mean much to me (he was right), that
Tommy had had six million units of penicillin and three
grams of streptomycin. Then he softened a bit and
explained that it seemed such a lot because it was meant to
last for twenty-four hours, whereas a normal human dose
is repeated every six hours. He told me to keep on with the
cough mixture, and to tempt Tommy's appetite with feeds
of equal quantities of oats and bran, salted to make it tasty,
and scalded with boiling water. I was to cool the feeds to
blood heat before offering them, testing them with my
elbow the way you do a baby's bath, and sprinkle brown
sugar on top to encourage the pony. But on no account must
the mash be allowed to get completely cold, or it would
taste sour. Tommy must also have all the water he could
drink.

After the vet had left I bought some bran from the corn

merchant, made up the feed in a bucket, and, while waiting for it to cool, built a manger in a corner of the toolshed because it might be easier for Tommy to eat at that height with his sore throat. Despite these preparations, very little of the food was eaten, the water wasn't touched, and neither was the fresh spring grass I brought in from the garden. I finished up the day lying in the straw by the pony's side, because he seemed to get some kind of comfort from the companionship.

The day after, Tuesday, was sunny and pretty and so warm that I thought it safe to tie Tommy up in the garden while I gave the toolshed a thorough mucking out. Despite the injections he still hadn't finished his feed, but when I went to bring him back into the toolshed I found him eating grass hungrily. I cut a trug-basket full to take into the stable, and Tommy ate it all. Encouraged by this, I fetched some more, and when I came back inside Tommy was lying down again. He ate half of the grass from my hand, but when I came to look at him later on I found him lying on the rest.

That afternoon the vet came again and Tommy had more injections. He still had a bit of a temperature, but it was lower, and the vet told me to take him out on a halter to graze whenever the weather was warm enough because he thought Tommy would prefer grass of his own choosing. By evening, Tommy was much more alert.

Next day he had obviously improved. He had nearly finished his feed and was for the first time willing to eat and drink off the floor while standing up. The sun was blazing down and the air temperature was up to 80°, so I led Tommy out on to the roadside to graze for half an hour. His eating habits were curious: though there was masses of rich grass to be had, he largely ignored it and picked

instead at bramble shoots, dandelions, and a host of other odd weeds. It seems that most horses and ponies will eat in this selective way, because the difference in mineral and protein content of each plant gives them a balanced diet. When we went back to the toolshed I took him loads of grass, and this time he ate it all eagerly.

The vet came again for the last time that evening. He thought Tommy was very much better, gave him a final couple of injections, and said that he wouldn't need to come again unless the pony got worse. Tommy's temperature was almost gone, and the vet thought he had recovered from his cold remarkably quickly. 'You can turn him out in the sun if the weather's fine,' he said, 'but bring him in at night. It's important not to let his coat get wet.'

It was at about this time that Tommy got his name (I have referred to him as Tommy so far because it was easier to use a name for him; but actually he still hadn't been given one, and had been called 'the pony'). A friend came over one evening to have a look at him, and she asked what he was called. He wasn't called anything, so we spent most of the rest of the evening thinking up a suitable name. I argued, since we didn't know the names of his sire and dam and were hardly likely to find them out, that he should be named for his breed (what breed?), and since he did not seem to be of Shetland origin (not stocky enough) and therefore probably had a fair amount of Welsh in him to account for his small size, I was in favour of a Welsh-sounding name. Not too Welsh, though, because the pony was obviously not a pure-bred. 'What about Thomas?' suggested my friend. 'It's a Welsh name, but there are lots of Thomases about who aren't Welsh.' So Thomas it was, and Tommy it became.

On the same evening we measured him, using a vertical bamboo cane for height and another laid horizontally across his withers, the bony bit in front of the saddle from which ponies' heights are taken. We made him 11.2 hands high (46"), which, give or take an inch or two for not using a proper measuring stick, was still very small.

Tommy went on improving, though frequent rain kept him in the toolshed for another eight days. In the intervals between the clouds – it was showery April-type weather, but with very heavy storms – we went out along the road-sides after grass. Traffic became less of a problem as Tommy got used to it, and soon he would not even raise his head unless a very heavy truck went past. The intimacy between us grew, though there was one incident in which I had to assert my superiority: I had been letting Tommy graze on quite a long piece of rope because it was easier for me to read my book if I didn't have to move every time he took a step, and it eventually happened that he got fed up, perhaps, of being followed around and kicked out at me sideways. Fortunately he got his foot over the lead-rope, and fortunately I happened to be paying attention. I snapped the rope tight, which shot his nose round sharply to the offending foot, and I held it there while I told him what I thought of him. He never tried to kick me again.

The relationship in the stable got better and better. Quite soon Tommy would whinny out when he heard me coming, and when he was lying down he would let me sit with him, or on him, or sprawl all over him without showing the slightest sign of fright or making an attempt to get up.

His winter coat was coming out fast, and he loved to have his coat scratched hard to get out the loose hairs. A good grooming every day helped.

It was time Tommy left the toolshed. He seemed to think so, too; and the tools were getting rusty.

After a week of confinement I was able to discontinue the cough medicine because Tommy showed no more signs of the disease, and I began to look about for a new field to put him in. I wanted to pasture him much nearer to my house, and no longer had to worry about putting him in with other horses because Tommy had become so friendly that he should be easy to catch. Cambridge, like most places, suffers from a shortage of grazing, and the field that I finally found had three ponies already there and not much grass on it. The rather lean grazing did not worry me much, because there was so much free grass to be had on the roadsides and I had come to enjoy my daily foragings with Tommy.

Chapter 5

THE MARKET PET, THE SHOWGROUND STAR

I had better admit that my methods of training Tommy were not the orthodox ones you would use for breaking a bigger pony or a horse. Since Tommy was so small, no matter what potential he showed for jumping or hunting he was almost bound to spend his life teaching a succession of very young children to ride. People who will treat a race-horse with the proper quiet respect will very often make no allowance for a small pony's nerves and will run up to him crying, 'Oh, what a sweet pony,' and try to put their arms around his neck. What Tommy needed to be was bomb-proof in traffic, kind and trustworthy enough for the most inexperienced child to handle, and able to put up with the most unreasonable happenings without turning a hair. For this reason, while I taught him to stand quietly to be groomed and to pick his feet up when requested, I also taught him to put up with me crawling about underneath him, sprawling on him when he was lying down, flapping dusters and umbrellas at him, running to him, and, ulti-mately, vaulting on over his backside. I wanted him to be prepared, if necessary, for the most inconsiderate child. Needless to say, these things took time.

The pony I turned out into the new field seemed quite

different from the one I had bought only three weeks before. He was more than easy to catch: he whinnied when I called him, and came to meet me. Out at exercise he followed me so readily and was so responsive to the voice that, on cross-country walks where there was no chance of meeting any traffic, I was tempted to let him follow loose and sometimes did, tying Tommy's lead-rope around his neck and leaving him to come along behind at his own pace. This gave him the freedom to pick his own bits of grazing; he would trot up after me to fall in behind, his nose not quite touching the small of my back, when he had finished his snack or when I felt I was leaving him too far behind and called to him to hurry up. In the early part of this training – if training is the right word; it was really more suitable behaviour for a dog than for a pony – I usually carried a box of Jaffa Cakes, which he loved, to encourage him.

Often we went into Cambridge, though Tommy was not allowed to run loose on the roads or in town. Grazing by the roadside when he had been convalescent had got him over his first fright with traffic, and quite soon it was possible to take Tommy through the Market Square at its busiest without his making any kind of fuss. Far from worrying about the people and the cars and bicycles, he became almost too friendly with the local stallholders, who were always pleased to see him and tended to spoil him. I did not think it fair to work him so soon after his illness, so these walks were meant only as a kind of general education in traffic and people and as a means of getting extra food to supplement the meagre grass on his field. I had to shop in Cambridge anyway, and as I did not want Tommy to forget such lessons as he had already been given about backing, I began to use

him as a pack pony for the groceries. We worked our way
round the market stalls, I buying fruit and vegetables and
Tommy getting free hand-outs of apples and carrots, with
pats and admiration from the stallholders, and then moved
on to the shops.

I had learned that the easiest way to unload the groceries after one of these trips was to take Tommy into the kitchen – Nif did not at all approve of this, and would climb on to the sideboard and chatter crossly at the pony – and unpack straight on to the table. When I was reasonably sure that he would behave himself indoors I began to take him into the shops with me; not all of the shops, of course, but the ones with friendly owners. Tommy was popular, and the shop owners made a fuss of him and gave him chocolate and peppermints. It came to an end quite quickly because I was afraid he would get spoilt. Besides, not everyone approved of Tommy in the Market Square – there was an old man who shouted, 'One way street,' whenever we went up a street the wrong way, rather as if he thought Tommy was a car – but most people were very glad to see him.

So much for the local character. By the end of May I was satisfied that Tommy was easy to catch and handle, safe in traffic, and well-behaved and friendly to strangers. On Whit Monday, May 29th, I had a chance to test all this at a horse show, which was held only a hundred yards from Tommy's field. I went down to the field early and caught him up, in case the unusual amount of cars and horses and people going past excited him. His summer coat was through and was beginning to shine, and I gave him a special polish to make him look his best. With constant brushing I had got his mane to lie down fairly neatly on the off side, and had trimmed the straggly ends of his tail. Because it was a formal occasion, I oiled his hooves for the show.

Looking back on it, I did some very silly things at that horse show and it is entirely to Tommy's credit that we did not have an accident. We went along to join the noisy, bustling mob of horses and ponies, treating it as if it were an everyday happening – yet only a month before Tommy had been completely wild. He behaved like a perfect gentleman: he stood at the ringside with me and watched the competitors for the jumping canter past; he walked and trotted along on his halter when I went to talk to friends of mine on ponies that he had never met. He didn't buck, or shy, or try to pull away from me, or get excited, and he

stood quietly by my side whenever I stopped to speak to
someone. All this went to my head. I think pride in Tommy
was understandable; but it quickly changed to foolishness
when two eleven-year-old girls, who were admiring him,
spoke to me at the ringside. I was admiring Tommy, too, so
we soon became friends. The girls had, they told me, been
breaking in ponies of their own, and they were interested to
hear how Tommy had been coming on. They were just what
I had been wishing I knew – keen, lightweight, experienced
young riders who were sensible and kind with my untaught
pony – and it wasn't long before the conversation got around
to talk of backing him, and of my regret that I was really
too heavy to ride him. Of course, they were very keen to
solve this problem, and just then we were joined by their
parents, who said certainly the girls could have a ride. So
up went the first one on to my hardly-backed and never-
ridden pony, whose only reaction was to put his ears back
nervously at her at first, and off we went round the edge of
the show ring, through all the strange ponies and people
and cars, with this unknown rider sitting there talking and
patting Tommy as if she had known him all her life.

Then the other girl had a turn, and so it went on for half
an hour. Tommy was perfectly relaxed and obedient, and I
got so proud and light-headed – and the girls did, too – that
when their little sister, aged six, said she thought it was
about her turn, none of us thought twice about putting her
up. What's so difficult about breaking a pony, I thought,
when I'm leading a happy six-year-old about on Tommy's
back?

Sometime during the afternoon, luckily before Tommy
became bored, reason returned and I took him home. He
had an extra feed that night; not that he needed it, as his

tummy was getting round and sleek on the good grass, but because he had behaved so extremely well. I lay in the grass by his head while he ate and told him so.

The day after that there was an unpleasant incident. Arriving at the field, I saw a spoilt little dog yapping round and round after the ponies. The owner stood by the gate looking lovingly at the fun her pet was having. 'Isn't he *naughty*,' she said to me, and she must have caught sight of the lead-rope I was carrying, or maybe it was the expression on my face that made her call out to the dog in a mock-severe voice, 'Mr Spanks will come.' And of course Mr Spanks didn't, so I went into the field and caught the nasty little thing a sharp one on the backside with the end of the lead-rope. It set up a frightful yelping, and so did its owner. She said something about calling the R.S.P.C.A., and I caught sight of the ponies bunched in the far corner of the field with their heads turned nervously towards us and got really furious and found myself shouting that if I ever saw that dog near my pony again, or near any other ponies, come to that, I'd bash its head in. An idle boast this, as it can't be easy to fulfil; but anyway owner and dog chose that moment to stalk off with dignity. This is the kind of dog that 'has fun' with a farmer's ewes at lambing time, or 'bravely' puts Magnificat up a tree, and when I saw the sweat round Tommy's ears and his nervous, flaring nostrils I would gladly have bashed its or its indulgent owner's head in if I had had the chance.

We went off across the fields together to walk it off. When we saw a gap in the hedge that looked low enough, we took to jumping.

Chapter 6

LUNGEING, LEARNING WORDS, LONG-REINING

In early June we jumped quite a lot. It wasn't an organized kind of jumping, but the cross-country sort that saved us from having to go round hedges and ditches. We scrambled through gaps together, and jumped hedges that were low enough for me to manage. There was never any question about Tommy's capabilities, nor was there about his enthusiasm, and soon he was going over obstacles alongside me instead of waiting to follow behind. On the quieter stretches of each walk I began to get on his back and ride. Though tall, I weighed only eight-and-a-half stone, which wasn't unreasonably heavy for him now that he was fit and well.

'Serious' jumping, for which Tommy was certainly not ready in the proper sequence of his training, began accident-ally. Someone put up a jumping pole on the stretch of grass outside his field, and the chance was too good to miss. We began by walking over the pole lying flat on the ground, then raised it to about ten inches, and subsequently raised it again to a foot-and-a-half. These heights were well within my scope, and Tommy enjoyed this sort of jumping-for-the-sake-of-it (as opposed to jumping to get somewhere) so much that I began to wonder whether I had a miniature show-jumper on my hands.

There was no question now that he was well and strong, and so there was no excuse for not having formal lessons. We began lungeing again in the second week of June, helped and advised by a friend called Grisel Hamilton, who had a lunge-whip. She also had a pretty, dappled-grey pony named Bimbi, who was pastured in Tommy's field and who was, it seemed from the amount of time they spent together at grass, Tommy's best friend.

It didn't start too well. I had had very little experience of lungeing, and, though I knew what I wanted Tommy to do, *he* didn't, and there was no assistant around to help me teach him. Fortunately Grisel came back from a ride on Bimbi just after the abortive lesson had begun, and burst out laughing when she saw me trying to get a perplexed Tommy to walk round me in circles. He kept coming up to me, looking for a pat and a bit of love, instead of keeping his distance at the end of the clothes line, and for the life of me I couldn't bring myself to hit him to keep him off. 'You're standing too far in front of him,' Grisel said. 'Hold on – I'll just put Bimbi away, and then I'll come and give you a hand.'

We tied another piece of rope to his headcollar on the far side – I had started with a rein only on the near side – and Grisel picked up the reins and the whip and stood behind him and a little to the left. 'Go on!' she shouted at him, sounding fierce, and I was horrified to hear the roughness in her voice and asked her to make it quieter because I did not want the pony frightened. 'Frighten *Tommy?*' Grisel said, laughing – she knew Tommy well and had a high opinion of his common sense – 'I couldn't frighten him if I tried. I'm only trying to get him to do a bit of work.'

She was quite right. She swore at Tommy again, and he, hearing the threat in her voice, took off at a canter, was checked by the reins, and began to canter round her in circles to the left, moving rather jerkily but following the guidance of her hand on the rope. 'Whoa,' said Grisel, after he had gone round her three times, and he gradually slowed up to a walk. We both of us patted and praised him, and then Grisel said, 'Here, you try,' and gave me the rope and her lunge-whip. I stood behind Tommy and slightly to the left and asked him to walk on. When he didn't, I used the tough tone that Grisel had taken and drew the whip lightly across his hindquarters (I don't think he knew what it was – probably he had never been whipped), and Tommy started forward at a trot. He was guided by the rein into a left-hand circle, and, with me standing at the centre but always keeping slightly behind him so that I could drive him on, trotted round me looking for all the world like an old hand at lungeing. He did a few circles, getting praise when he did his best, and exhortations to go on, backed up with a slow swing of the whip towards his quarters, when he looked like stopping, and after half-a-dozen circles I thought I had better stop him while he was still going well. I tried saying,

'Whoa,' but he didn't understand the word, so I dropped the whip and moved a pace or two forward so that I was slightly in front of him instead of behind, and he stopped and turned to look at me.

We lunged every day after that, never working for more than a quarter of an hour because lungeing can get boring. Ponies are like humans in that they appear to be right- or left-handed, or right- or left-sided, as it is called. Tommy was quite markedly left-sided; in a tight corner he always turned to the left, and he was much easier to lead to the left than to the right (to help counteract this I often used to lead him from the off side). A good riding pony must learn to be ambidextrous, turning to the right or left with equal ease, so most of Tommy's work on the lunge was done on the right rein (or clothes line – I still hadn't got the proper tack) to teach him to be more flexible on that side.

As Tommy worked more to the right hand than to the left his balance seemed to improve and he moved more easily to the right, though it was still easier to get him to lunge to the left. I supplemented the teaching by getting him to walk, trot, and whoa on his halter when we were out for exercise, so that he came to associate the words with the actions. Animals can be taught a very elementary vocabulary, as I had learned from Nif, who knew about ten words and short phrases such as 'Good', 'Yes', 'No', 'Beef', 'Kittens', 'Look', 'Bad cat', 'Pig', and 'Kill the moth', though it seemed to be the tone of voice rather than the actual word that was listened to. 'Pig' was the least successful word because, though I meant it rudely, Nif understood it as a term of affection and would produce one of her huge cat-smiles and hold up her head to be kissed every time it was used. 'Beef', however, which was Nif's favourite food and was fed to her raw with great ceremony, was always anxiously listened for and words like 'leaf', or 'teeth' coming up naturally in conversations, would often provoke her into climbing on my lap with a happy, expectant look when I hadn't in fact been talking to her.

Tommy's vocabulary included 'Walk', 'Trot', 'Stand', 'Get over', 'Pick it up' (for feet), 'Thomas' (used reproachfully), 'No', 'Good boy', and, ultimately, 'Canter'. I rode him for a little while every day, and when I was sure he understood

the voice commands I gave him I began to use gentle leg and hand aids at the same time to get him to associate the new pressures with the words.

Long-reining began about this time. This is driving the pony from behind with a rein attached to his headcollar on either side, and it teaches him to obey signals on the reins which will later be given from the saddle. It also teaches him, since there is someone behind him telling him to get on with it, to walk out well and to walk up into his bridle (or headcollar). The reins running along either side of the pony's body are useful, too, because you can get him to walk straight and clean between them instead of crabbing about sideways or walking out of true.

But you have to remember to keep the reins fairly short

or you can get into a muddle. Sometimes I got into an awful mess with the reins, and needed help to get them straightened out.

So the first two weeks of June went by: a little lungeing, a little long-reining, walks through traffic, walks across country with an occasional small jump, a hundred yards or more of being ridden, daily grooming and handling of his feet. Tommy got fatter and sleeker, and I got thinner. And all the time he got more confident and more obedient and responsive. He was a most rewarding pony to train: he enjoyed his lessons – you could tell from the way he whinnied out and trotted to meet me each day, and from the way he hung around the gate when I turned him out.

On June 15th I went to the saddler's and bought him a bridle.

Chapter 7

A BIT ON THE SIDE

Tommy's first bridle, which was not a success, had a rubber bit. I bought it because I thought it would be the best way to protect his delicate mouth, but it seems that rubber bits only come in one size, and when I opened his mouth and slipped it in I found that his head was far too tiny and his jaws couldn't close over the rubber. I took the bit back and bought, instead, a jointed snaffle, made of thick metal because the thinner ones tend to pinch the pony's mouth. Ideally, I would have liked to buy a breaking bit with 'players' on it – little lumps of metal attached to the centre of the bit so that the pony is encouraged to play with them with his tongue and quickly gets the feel of a bit in his mouth – but this, as usual, was too expensive. But I did buy a couple of circular pieces of rubber, which I fitted on to the bit on each side to prevent the bit rings from chafing the corners of his soft mouth.

On June 16th, after we had been out for exercise, I slipped Tommy's snaffle into his mouth, pulled the headpiece up over his ears, straightened out his forelock, and adjusted the cheek pieces on the bridle so that the bit rested on the bare gums between his front and back teeth and just wrinkled the corners of his mouth. Then I put the headcollar back over the bridle. Tommy did not seem to mind: he swung his head up and down a couple of times, playing with the curious new thing in his mouth, and accepted a toffee from me (sounding, as he chinked it about with the bit, as if he was turning it into a sticky mess). We went for a walk round the field while Tommy thought about what he had in his mouth – you could see him playing with the bit with his tongue – and after ten minutes, when he no longer seemed interested in his bridle, I took it off him and turned him out. After that I made him wear the bridle and the headcollar at exercise, giving him most of his instructions on the headcollar rope but also gently using the reins, when mounted, to get him to follow the bit as well. At first, when I used the bridle, I rode on what they call an 'open rein', holding my guiding arm out to the side so that the sideways pull on Tommy's mouth gave him a clearer indication of which way to turn.

For the past few weeks I had been looking out for a rider who was experienced enough to handle a complete novice and was also light enough to ride him. I had a stroke of luck when I met Louise Wallace, an excellent young horse-woman, eleven years old and weighing only $4\frac{1}{2}$ stone. On June 19th Louise came for her first ride on Tommy. Both of us were confident that he was ready to be ridden alone, and here I learned that I had misjudged my training of him. Much as Nif paid attention to the word 'beef' (or 'leaf', come to that) if *I* said it, Tommy, whom I had lately been finding easy to ride, didn't seem to associate Louise's leg and hand aids with mine. He was obviously difficult to stop and turn, and the ungainly way he carried himself suggested that he could do with a lot more lungeing. Rather than give in, which would have been bad for discipline, Louise and I solved the immediate problem by taking Tommy for a walk.

She, mounted, gave the correct aids as I gave him the voice commands that he was used to, and this seemed to work well enough. It was difficult, however, to tell whether Tommy was actually learning anything.

We tried it again a few times, with Louise riding Tommy when I lunged him and sometimes coming along on our walks, but we could both see that he did not really understand what she wanted of him and so we decided to wait awhile for lessons, such as jumping, where Louise would be really indispensable (I was much too heavy), and let me get on with the elementary school work myself.

Every day, after a few minutes on the lunge, Tommy and I went into Cambridge or took off across country. Out in the fields where there was no one about I used often to let Tommy run loose. When I did this, I tied the lead-rope around his neck and unbuckled and removed the reins so that he did not get his feet caught in them. He became fonder and fonder of jumping; I would ride him across a field until we got to the hedge or ditch on the other side, then dismount and take off Tommy's reins at a place where it was easy for me to climb through. Then, depending on our

moods, either I would climb over first or Tommy would bound on ahead and wait for me on the other side. He was always very sensible about obstacles such as barbed wire.

Once I tried long-reining him over a small hedge, but he went at it much too fast for me and, as I was forced to jump the thing rather than climb it, I gave up that idea right away. On one of these walks we got lost and had to make our way back over three miles or more of country that I didn't know, and it was then that I realized how very versatile a small pony is, because there were no obstacles in our path that Tommy couldn't manage to find a way through somehow.

Often we schooled up and down a steep gully by the field, Tommy on long reins, because the direct descent and ascent meant he had to gather his body together and get his hocks under him, and this improved his carriage.

Every other day we went out for exercise with Grisel and Bimbi. Bimbi was beautifully behaved, and I hoped that

working with him would improve Tommy's manners. We did cross-country and road work together, sometimes with Grisel leading Tommy from Bimbi's back so that he should learn to be led from another horse. I rode him when he was being led to give extra control. I was riding him now every day, usually for about half of our hour-and-a-half exercise, getting off fairly frequently to give his back a rest. He carried me easily, sometimes breaking for a few strides into a canter.

Tommy's field was fenced with concrete posts and four strands of tightly strung plain wire. It had a stream running along one end of it, and bushes on the stream bank gave shade and a place to get out of the flies on a hot day. Though there wasn't much grass on the field I was surprised to see that Tommy, in contrast to the other ponies, was getting fatter and fatter. One morning I learned why: I had gone down to the field extra early, as I was going to London at lunchtime, and there was Tommy lying down on the rich grass outside the field. He looked, I thought, a bit smug. None of the other ponies was out. Mystified, I made a careful check of the fencing, which was perfect, although on the far side of the stream in the bushes only three strands of wire had been strung. I gave Tommy his workout and turned him out. Next day when I came to fetch him, there he was again – waiting at the gate for me as usual, but *outside it.*

I worked him that day for less than the usual time, and when I turned him out he was still fresh and did not want to be left. I walked along the fence, keeping on the outside, and when we got to the stream at the end I kept on away from the field. Tommy turned away at a trot and went to the far end of the stream, where the banks were less steep. 'Come on, Tom,' I called, wanting to see what he would do. He splashed down the shallow stream bed towards me, turned by the bridge where I had crossed, stuck his head under the lowest of the three strands of wire and with a wriggle was through and coming towards me, very pleased with himself. He even did a little buck to show off. What do you do with a pony like that?

This was the beginning of Tommy's perfect freedom. I became used to the daily sight of three healthy-looking ponies grazing on a field of lean grass, and the fourth, much too fat, snoozing in the sun on the bright green sward outside the gate. Tommy's field was down a quarter of a mile of drive, and I never really worried that he would go towards the traffic because the country behind the field was open and was much more interesting for a pony. Sometimes I would find him in his field, looking demure, but I was sure that he had been out during the night and had only gone back in to chat to his friends. After a while I didn't even bother to put him in the field.

Chapter 8

WINGS IN HIS HEART
AND IRON ON HIS FEET

On July 8th I had my first decent canter on Tommy, sitting
tight and holding on to the mane because he was feeling so
well that I was afraid there might be trouble. There was:
after a few strides he put his head down and bucked like a
little bronco. If a horse bucks with you and you come down
in the right position on the first buck, it is thereafter often
difficult for him to shake you off. Luckily this happened
with Tommy, and luckily he chose to buck in a straight line,
which is much easier to sit (the kinks and twists of a horse
that starts off bucking to the side are murderous); so, instead
of pulling his head up to stop him from bucking, I let him
buck as much and as long as he liked because, in my
experience, young horses who have a real go at their riders
and are unsuccessful seem to forget about bucking as a way
of getting free and will later only put in the occasional buck
out of pure high spirits. Tommy, anyway, went quite rigid,
and pitched and gallumphed along with great exuberance
with me hanging on tightly, until he had got it out of his
system and slowed and stopped. Both of us were out of
breath. He turned his head, with widely flaring nostrils,
round to me, as much as to say, 'Are you still there?', and
never did it again. But I was lucky. I can't recommend this

as a safe way to teach a young horse not to buck, because if I had come unstuck Tommy would have learned a very naughty lesson.

It's time for a recap: Tommy, after ten weeks of training, was a pleasure to catch and handle. He was fun to groom, though sometimes he ate my hair or fidgeted about, and he didn't like having his nose cleaned. He held up each foot when asked, moved over on command, would let me crawl about under him or sit on him when he was lying down. He was perfect in traffic. He obeyed me exactly, though he was still rattled by the occasional inexperienced child I found watching, rapt, by the field, and to whom I gave pony rides. He lunged and long-reined as required, was excellent across country, and seemed to be a natural jumper.

On the bad side, it was impossible to keep him in his field (he was blasé enough now to walk openly through all four strands of wire, putting his foot on the lowest strand and pushing under the next), and worse, he was getting bossy habits from the horses he was pastured with; though much the smallest, he insisted on getting his own way, and tended to push the others around and nip at them. He had still never worn a saddle, nor had he been shod.

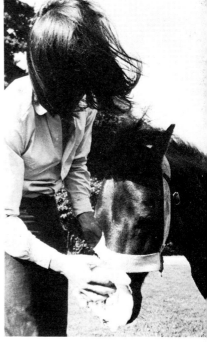

I planned next to regulate his jumping. The local riding school had an indoor school and an abundant supply of cavaletti, which are single poles fixed at each end to wooden crosses. By turning the crosses upside-down, sideways, or right-way-up, pole heights of about ten inches, fifteen inches, and nineteen inches can be obtained (a close look at the cavaletti in the photograph below shows how), so that you can get a variety of small jumps out of one cavaletti. Cavaletti can also be stacked together to give a jump of good height and spread, or can be placed separately at intervals to make the pony lengthen or shorten his stride to get over them, and teach him to judge his jumps. I didn't think we would have much trouble with this phase of the education because Tommy liked jumping so much, but Grisel and I agreed that it might be a good idea to take the more experienced Bimbi along to the school to set an example.

We set up some of the cavaletti as a guard rail to keep the ponies near the wall of the school, and we made a few jumps at the lowest height in our roughly constructed jumping lane. We reckoned the jumps were just about big enough to make the ponies break their stride. I took the reins off Tommy's bridle, and Grisel loosed Bimbi and said, 'Right, here we go,' and called out to her well-trained pony to get on with it. They didn't need telling – they went off round the closed school like the clappers, having a marvellous time over the little fences, and the only thing wrong with it was that Tommy led and Bimbi, the trained jumper, followed.

'Here,' I said to Grisel, 'we'd better catch yours and try to give mine a lesson in discipline.' So we stopped Bimbi, and I took Tommy out alone over the little fences, moving up and inside him with the lunge-whip; and the only difficulty I had with him was keeping up. Tommy had tremendous

fun: he jumped cavaletti one at a time, and then he jumped two set fourteen feet apart, which made him break his stride and take a canter step in between; he jumped them at intervals of nine feet, which made him think what he was doing. He jumped two cavaletti together, to make him stretch, as he had with Bimbi. Finally he jumped a pile of three of them, which made him stretch even more.

It was a lot to cram into a first lesson. It would have been wiser to have spread it out over three or four stages, and I excuse it because I didn't often have the opportunity to use cavaletti, and because Tommy was not really a complete novice over jumps. A real first-time-over-any-sort-of-jump pony ought to have a first lesson over poles laid flat on the ground. I stopped Tommy at last because he was becoming over-excited (excitement can teach a pony to rush his fences, and I didn't want him to make a silly mess of one of his jumps), and we took the two happy ponies away from the school long before their enthusiasm had faded.

On July 16th Tommy broke into Grisel's stable, just outside the field, and ate Bimbi's bridle. I tried telling Grisel that this was funny, but she said it was only funny if I paid for the repairs.

His wanderings got worse, though he always came back to his field in time for exercise. It was a fine summer, hot after a wet spring, and the crops were tall and beginning to ripen. Once in a while, strangers who noticed me carrying a bridle would stop me to ask if I knew of anyone who owned a small bay pony, as one had been seen in a field of corn three miles or so away. I learned that the safest answer to this was, 'No.'

The day after the bridle-eating incident, to which I had had to own up, provided the narrowest squeak we had. Most of the land round about belonged to Lord Rothschild, who seemed to have a very understanding attitude towards young ponies; at any rate, neither he nor his staff complained to me about Tommy, though they must have known whose the pony was.

On the morning of July 17th, after breakfasting on Lord Rothschild's barley, Tommy turned sociable and paid a visit to his lordship's groundsman. The gate to the groundsman's cottage happened to be open, so Tommy trotted cheerfully up the garden path to the front door. The groundsman's wife, who was expecting a visitor, heard him coming, and I heard later that she took off her apron before answering the door.

Since I was unable to make him stay in his field, I thought that a possible solution to his persistent trespassing might be to tire him out with work each day so that he was more inclined to stay at home. We went for long cross-country rides, and often into town through the heaviest traffic. Sometimes we jumped in the covered school, or over a pole set up outside the field. Before each exercise I made Tommy work on the lunge, or long-reined him up and down the gully. His balance, carriage, and flexibility improved a lot, and so did the muscles in my legs.

As the work was beginning to wear down his feet, I took advantage of the farrier's regular visits to Bimbi and asked him to put a set of shoes on Tommy. I didn't expect trouble because the man shod the ponies cold when he was away from his forge, and the only problem we had was that the nails were the wrong size for such a tiny pony and the shoes could have been a better fit. Shoeing a pony with badly-fitting shoes seems to me worse than not shoeing it at all, so we arranged instead that I would take Tommy to the forge on August 9th, a day when the smith would be at home all morning, and have hot shoes fitted.

The forge was about three miles away on the other side of Cambridge, and I wondered as I led Tommy through the traffic how he would react to the smell of his own hooves burning, and what he would think of the return journey with his new shoes ringing on the tarmac. I warned the farrier that the pony had never been shod hot, and both of us braced ourselves for the kind of struggle you get when a pony smells singeing hoof for the first time. Tommy stood quietly tied up in the forge while the smith heated up lengths of iron and cut and bent them into tiny horseshoes, explaining as he worked that there was a steel strike on and light iron was not available and that, though he was using the lightest iron he had, it would be a bit heavy for such a small pony. When he had the first shoe roughly made he brought the red-hot piece of iron over to try it for fit on Tommy's hoof. I untied Tommy because I was afraid he might pull back and snap his lead-rope, and stood close up against his neck to try to stop too much of the smoke from the burning hoof from drifting into his face and frightening him. I put an arm round his neck and talked into his ear, and Tommy held up his foot for the smith and was so far from being frightened that he didn't even cock his ears nervously when the hot shoe sizzled against his hoof.

The surprised farrier took the shoe away for small adjustments, plunged it into a tub of cold water, and nailed it into place on Tommy's foot. Then, with equal ease, he shod the other three feet. When he had finished – had turned over the ends of the nails, now sticking through Tommy's hooves, so that the pony couldn't snag himself, and rasped down the rough outer wall of each foot to get it neatly in line with the new shoes – he paid Tommy a great compliment. 'I don't care what you say,' he said, 'that pony's never only three years old.' So I lifted back Tommy's lips to show his teeth and prove it, and I got a nasty shock: there was a missing tooth in the lower set of Tommy's front jaw, and the gum round it was swollen and bruised. It looked as if one of the ponies he was pastured with had kicked him in the mouth, but he had given no sign of pain when I had put his bridle on that morning. I took the bit out of his mouth and rode him home in his headcollar, feeling beastly, and just before we got to the field Tommy half shied at a building crane which swung round towards us dripping earth and his near fore shoe fell off. It seemed that the iron at the end of the shoe had not been bent round far enough to the shape of the foot and was sticking out behind a bit, so that Tommy must have stepped on it and pulled it off. The last hundred yards home he went clop, clop, clop, *plunk*. Next day the smith came over, adjusted the shoe and nailed it back on again.

I didn't ride Tommy in a bridle again until August 21st, a week after the bruises and the swelling in his mouth had disappeared, and by that time I had managed to borrow a tiny saddle and Tommy had got used to wearing it.

Chapter 9

TOMMY TEACHER

I can't say that Tommy was any too keen on the saddle at first, as it was the first time that anything had been strapped round his middle. It is not so much the weight of the thing – heaven knows, Tommy had been carrying the groceries and me for long enough – but the feeling of constriction, which will often upset a pony who is girthed up for the first time. An unhandled pony will usually try to buck the strange thing off, and may panic when it finds it can't, so I was careful to introduce Tommy gradually to the new piece of saddlery by doing up the girths only just tight enough to hold the saddle in place, not tight enough to cause him any discomfort. He flicked his ears around and squinted at it nervously when he took his first few steps wearing it and felt for the first time the queer constricting thing round his belly. But he took it very well, and soon he was trotting about daily with the stirrups flapping loose against his sides (though I didn't let him run loose like that because it wasn't my saddle).

I began to teach him the turn on the forehand, the swing of the hindquarters to right or left while the front feet remain stationary, that is so useful out hunting when you are trying to get the side of the pony closer to the latch of the gate. It is no good trying to teach this unless the pony is responsive to the bit and to the leg aids. I started by asking Tommy to make a forehand turn to the left, which was still his supplest side, and got him to stand squarely on all four feet before I gently pulled on the left rein to bring his head round slightly, slid my left leg back a bit to push his quarters over to the right, and kept up a light pressure at the girth with my right leg to stop him from walking backwards. Tommy was at first stubborn about this, but weight and strength once again were on my side and at the third time of asking he did it – or happened to do it. Never mind the reason; if the pony does as requested and gets praise when he does it, he will soon learn what the peculiar new leg and hand signals mean. I only asked for two steps round with the hind legs, not wanting to overdo it at the start, and then patted him and walked him forward.

The fine weather held, and by mid-August the harvest was mostly in. Tommy went well for me on our rides across the fields of stubble, answering to my signals on the headcollar rein as well as many ponies would to the bridle. I taught him to neck-rein, to turn away from the pressure of the rope against his neck so that he could be ridden one-handed. I did this by turning him, for example, to the right with the usual feel on the right rein plus pressing the left rein gently across his neck and leaning to the right, and gradually stopped using the right rein at all. After a while I could control him with a single rein on the headcollar instead of one on each side of his neck.

I didn't ride him in the saddle because it was too small for me, so Muffet Hamilton, Grisel's eleven-year-old daughter, did the work from the saddle. She schooled Tommy for me fairly often, riding him in circles and figures of eight to get him balanced and perfectly responsive. Sometimes she took him out by herself for a ride, and I was quite surprised when one day she reported that he was difficult to stop. My first response to this was a surge of pride that the pony, *my* pony, responded perfectly only to me – the thing that I had always wanted as a child was a pony who had a perfect rapport only with me, preferably one that no one else could ride. But I saw how stupid this was: what chance would Tommy have of a happy future, and what use would he be, unless he was a good, safe ride for anyone who came along? This meant *anyone*, beginners included, so I looked around for a young child who wanted to learn and came up with Donald, a seven-year-old American who was about to have his first lessons in riding from a friend of mine called Annice Morrison.

On August 21st, the day that I thought Tommy's mouth sound enough to have the bit back in, I went down to the field at ten o'clock to fetch him. Grisel and Muffet, who had had Bimbi out for an early school, were there grinning at me. It emerged that they had had to put Tommy back into the field twice since eight-thirty, though he had artfully not let them see the way he got out. I gave the little fellow a good grooming and rode him barebacked over to Annice's place, where she had told me there was a small saddle we could use.

Donald turned out to be awfully small and awfully keen and completely inexperienced. He jumped around with excitement – Annice told him people must be quiet and calm with ponies, and I was glad of the time I had put in bouncing about with Tommy and squeaking at him – while Tommy stood patiently and we saddled him up. Donald let out an 'Oooh' of pleasure when Annice lifted him into the saddle, and grabbed hold of the reins and kicked the pony's sides (fortunately I was holding on to Tommy's head). Annice showed Donald how to sit and how to hold the reins so that he didn't pull on Tommy's mouth, and then, since he said he was fine and he certainly didn't want to be held, she led him off in a circle round the paddock.

It wasn't very successful. Donald, though keen and brave and blissfully unaware that he might quite easily fall off if he didn't watch it, held the reins rigidly like the novice he was – he hadn't yet learned, of course, that his hands must move with the rhythmic sway of the pony's head. He seemed to think the reins were only something to hold on by, and the awkward way he sat on the saddle made Tommy nervous and flustered. I watched the pony's ears flicking worriedly back and forth and saw the anxious way he pushed at Annice with his nose, wanting to give the orders because he wasn't confident that the situation was in control, and thought that we had better stop before he or Donald got upset. We didn't, however, want to discourage Donald, who was quite unaware that anything was wrong, and we – or I, at least – also wanted to teach Tommy that it was perfectly safe and normal to carry a novice rider. Donald's seat on Tommy had looked most unsafe. He sat as if he was perched on a chair, and expected the chair not to move, so the first thing we did was take off Tommy's saddle and lift Donald on to his bare back. That way, we thought, he would be able to feel the way the pony's muscles moved, and he would have to pay attention to the way he was sitting because if he relaxed too much or sat over to one side he might easily slip off. We unbuckled one of the stirrup leathers and fastened it around Tommy's neck, telling Donald to hold on to that, as it was too much to expect him to learn how to sit and also how to hold the reins on his very first pony-ride.

Loosed from the novice clutch on the reins, and not at all unhappy with the tiny figure sitting proud and straight on his furry back, Tommy settled down at once. I led him around the paddock for a bit, turning this way and that so that Donald could feel the slight differences in balance, while Annice walked beside us with a hand on Donald's leg and gave him a lesson in how to sit. She was very good at this: she soon had Donald sitting responsively instead of slackly, and she did it with such tact that he got more and more keen to be a rider and much more confident and easy. After a quarter of an hour I thought we had better stop, because I didn't want Tommy to get bored and anyway Donald had absorbed quite as much as could be expected from a first lesson, so we lifted Donald down and I rode Tommy around the paddock to get him responsive and interested again (ponies can get lazy and fed up if they are led slowly about while someone has a lesson on them).

Annice, who was keen on show-jumping, had a set of cavaletti in her paddock, which made a good opportunity for a short lesson for Tommy. I trotted him over them, on foot of course, in various positions and heights, while Donald stood by and watched and asked how long it would be before he, too, could jump.

All this was very encouraging – both Tommy and Donald seemed to be learning something, and Annice and I were enjoying it – and so we arranged that Tommy and I would come back the next day for another lesson.

The following morning I came up against one of the slight snags that can crop up when you have your pony pastured with others. The riding school who owned Tommy's grazing had had to increase the number of ponies in his field to six, and three of them were being caught when I went to fetch him. There was a great deal of galloping about and bucking and whinnying, and Tommy, when he came to me, was excited and flustered. I waited until the hoof-noises of the ponies who had been caught had faded away up the track, and then I rode him in circles at a walk and a trot, changing diagonal frequently, until he had calmed down. I had become so accustomed to Tommy's calm good sense that I had almost forgotten that he was only three and liable to get excited, and this small reminder was good for me.

There was another reminder on the way over to Annice's. The path across the fields ran past the Cambridge School of Veterinary Medicine, which stocked all sorts of animals needed for research and animal husbandry. The worst of these, from the pony's point of view, were pigs. I have no idea why ponies dislike pigs, but it seems to be true of most of them and Tommy was no exception. The wind blew the farmyard and medical smell towards us as we approached, and most strongly on the wind came the smell of pigs. Tommy hated it: he got very tense under me and stopped and tried to turn back. I wouldn't let him, keeping him straight with the reins and with a firm pressure with the legs. Since he could not turn, poor Tommy tried to run backwards away from the frightful smell, so I slapped him on the rump with an open hand and told him not to be silly.

I think, rightly or wrongly, that there is a point in this sort of situation where a pony is apprehensive without being really frightened, and that he can almost be laughed out of it if his rider is ready for it. Once the pony has turned to get away, or the rider has decided that the pony has a point and has dismounted to lead him past, then the suspicion is confirmed and there is likely to be a fight whenever that smell is encountered in the future. Ponies have excellent memories, and pigs, no matter how diabolical they may smell to some, are often met with. Anyway, I talked to Tommy and patted him and urged him to go forward, and pretty soon he went by, his neck arched and stiff, walking as it seemed on tiptoe. When we were past the worst of it I told him how brave and good he was.

Donald and Annice were waiting for us, and Donald let out a yell of pleasure and rushed to meet Tommy and got soundly told off by both of us. It did nothing to stint his enthusiasm, though it quietened him down, and soon he was up on the bare back, holding on tight to the stirrup leather round Tommy's neck and trying to remember how to sit like a horseman. Annice and I thought it would be more fun if we actually went somewhere instead of going round and round the paddock, so we went out for a mile and a half across the fields, which were nearly all stubble at that time of year. It was a perfect day, hot with a deep blue sky and skylarks all over the place, and when in one of the fields we came across some bales of straw left from the harvest we took Donald off for a moment and led Tommy over one of them at a trot. When he had jumped it perfectly from both sides we stopped.

Tommy and I went home on the A45 in heavy traffic and reached my house in Cambridge just before lunchtime. We took a short cut round to the back of the house across a newly harvested field of wheat. Coming off the main road there were gaps in the hedge. We left the rumbling, draughty lorries behind and cantered across the stubble to the far side of the field, where we were stopped by a deep ditch overgrown with rose bay willowherb. I dismounted and scrambled over, but Tommy would not follow me until he had eaten most of the willowherb that grew out of his side of the ditch.

At home I turned him loose in the back garden, where the grass in the tiny orchard grew thick, and went in to get my own lunch. Nif saw the pony from the dining-room window and complained to me again. I followed her gaze outside: Tommy was running about all over the flower beds. I went outside and tied him up.

Chapter 10

A VERY NASTY HORSE

Early in the afternoon it rained quite heavily from what seemed to be a clear blue sky. The sun shone through the dripping air, and there was a rainbow at the bottom of the garden (though not, I supposed, a crock of gold). Nif went to the back door and asked to go out, and since 'Rain' was not one of the words in her vocabulary I opened the door to show her what was happening. Her eager little face clouded and she looked quite despondent, but then she perked up and led me off to see if it was raining outside the front door. Then we tried the side door out of the dining-room, the french windows in the drawing-room, and so on round all of the windows on the ground floor, Nif leading me and never going to the same place twice. It was, of course, raining outside each opening, as I had learned it would be before I was old enough to wonder why; but Nif's reasonable attitude that because it was raining outside one door did not mean that it would be raining outside the others, a sort of Nif-Through-the-Looking-Glass concept that had never crossed my mind, remained with me for the rest of the day, and was, I thought, a highly intelligent bit of logic for a cat.

When the shower had stopped I trotted Tommy back to

his field, running alongside him because he was far too wet to sit on. Grisel was catching up Bimbi for an afternoon ride. I put Tommy into the field and gave him some sweet, early Worcesters, and he did not want to be turned out but stayed with us while Bimbi was being saddled up.

He left us for a minute or two to have a roll. I watched as he went over and over, his neck stretched out to scratch as much as possible of his person in the damp grass. Finally he finished and decided to get up. He was much too fat to make it on the first attempt, but got his forelegs up straight and

sat on his bottom looking at us with his huge paunch spreading over his hind feet. Grisel and I burst out laughing at him, although it wasn't very polite, and, still chuckling, I walked off along the fence to fetch my bike, which I had left hidden at the far end of the field beyond the stream. Tommy trotted across the field to his favourite way out, cantered along the stream bed, ducked under the wire, and joined me just as I crossed the bridge. He fell into step behind me, walking along in his usual fashion with his nose not quite touching the small of my back.

If he was really determined to get out, I thought I had better clean out the old water bath that lay on the open piece of ground behind the field, which I did. Tommy had a drink,

then went to the gate of the big field next to his and leaned over it with his ears pricked. About twenty of the riding school's horses and ponies were pastured there, and Tommy seemed keen to join them. So, rather than leave him to find his own way in, which could easily mean a new hole in the hedge, I opened the gate and let him in. He cantered off to make friends, and from then on seldom strayed out of his pasture.

The big new field was really four fields knocked into one, with the remains of unkept hedges roughly dividing it up and a spinney over towards the farthest corner. I did not realize its disadvantages the first time I went to catch Tommy there, because all I did was lean over the gate and call and he whinnied back from behind one of the hedges and came up to me at a canter. I rode round the boundaries of the field on his back and was glad that the stream ran through it, but worried to see that the fence at the most distant corner of the field was a single strand of sagging wire that could hardly have held in any pony – let alone Tommy

– who wanted to get out. But there was plenty of grass and shade, and plenty of company. Much too much company, as it turned out.

In the heat of the following day I went to fetch Tommy and was disconcerted to find that there wasn't a pony in sight. I called, but there was no reply, so I walked what seemed an endless distance across the field to the spinney, where I found them all under the trees in the shade, standing head to tail and flicking the flies off each other with their tails. Tommy's companion at this was a big bay mare called Bess who was a half-bred carthorse, and I could not at all understand the attraction between them because the difference in their size and bulk was ludicrous. Bess, though, was far from being a humorous sort of horse. She seemed to have formed an attachment for Tommy, and she followed behind as Tommy came to meet me. In the next few days I was to learn that the passion was mutual and that the two unlikely animals were pretty well inseparable.

Of all the rude things I can think of to say about Bess, stupid is not one of them. When she saw that I was carrying a lead-rope and meant to take her new pet away, she came past Tommy in a rush and went for me with her ears flat back and the whites of her eyes showing. There was no doubt that she meant business, so I dodged behind a tree and called to Tommy to come and get me out of it. Luckily he did, and once I was on his back Bess did not try to interfere, though Tommy was most unwilling to leave this hideous horse behind and go off for exercise without her.

He forgot her, fickle little chap, as soon as we were out of the field, and went off in great spirits for the day's lesson. This time, with the help of lightweight Louise Wallace, it was jumping in the covered school with a rider on his back.

I let him run round over the cavaletti loose for a couple of minutes to refresh his memory, and then we saddled him up and Louise got on. She had excellent hands and a sensible and intelligent attitude, and she realized that the most important thing initially was not to interfere with Tommy when he jumped, but merely to adapt her balance so that her weight (if $4\frac{1}{2}$ stone can be called a weight) did not make things difficult for him. At first she let him go over the cavaletti at its lowest height, keeping him to a trot so that all he had to do was break his stride over the pole. I followed along to give Tommy the feeling that this was a normal jumping session, but then I backed off to the centre of the school and let Louise take him along herself. Each time he jumped well she patted him, and on the odd occasion when he misjudged it she didn't take him to task but simply trotted

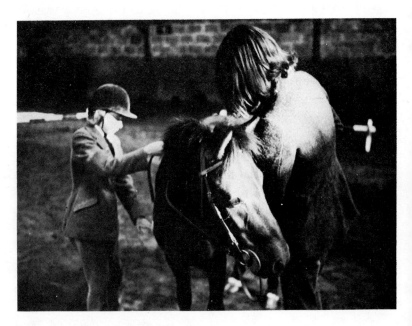

him on round the school and got it right next time. After five minutes of this she squeezed him into a canter and had him going round like an old hand, although it was necessary for her to slow him up after each jump so that he was not allowed to rush.

We thought that was enough for the first day, and stopped it while we were all still pleased and confident. I took Tommy home, and, not having any liking for the monster

Bess, turned him out in his old paddock. But he had no intention of staying there: he did not even bother to get out by his roundabout way through the stream, but followed me along the wire as I went to fetch my bike and at the end of the field simply put a foot on the lowest strand, ducked his head under the strand above that, and walked blatantly through the fence as if it had never been intended to keep ponies in. He walked along behind me until he saw that I was picking up the bike and meant to go home, and then he went to the gate of the new field and called longingly to the horrible great mare who was grazing nearby. So I gave in and let him in, hoping that when I next came to catch Tommy some brave person would have taken his friend out for a ride.

Luck was with me for a couple of days – it was the weekend, when most riding school animals have to earn their keep – but on the next Monday beastly Bess got a day of rest. There are hardly any horses who will deliberately hurt anyone, but those that will have a special sort of feel about them so that they seem to radiate trouble without necessarily giving any outward signs of it. Once, when exercising regularly for a racehorse trainer, I was told to saddle up the horse in the third box down whom I was to ride that morning. I had not been on his back before, but had noticed him at exercise and thought what a well-behaved sort he was. So, glad that I had a nice ride that day, I opened the door of the loosebox and walked in, pulling the door shut behind me. The horse turned to meet me, his ears pricked and a mild and interested expression in his eyes, and for no reason that I could think of I dropped the tack and was out of the box at top speed, bolting the door behind me. 'Anything up?' called the trainer. I said, feeling foolish, that under no circumstances would I saddle that horse. 'Been up to his tricks already, has he?' said the trainer, who was one of the most lion-hearted men with a horse I have ever met. 'He almost had me yesterday. I went in to give him his feed, and he waited until he was between me and the door and then he went for me. I only just made it up into the rafters, and he kept me treed up there for two hours before a couple of the lads came along and drew him off.' He seemed to think it funny, but it was not a joke that appealed to me. That chestnut racer frightened me, and so, also rightly, did a thoroughbred stallion whom I watched bucking about in his field. The only other horse who ever gave me the feeling was Bess.

Anyway, on that Monday I wanted Tommy; and to get him, since he was out of earshot on the other side of the field, I had to go into the field with Bess. Not wanting to provoke her I kept as quiet as possible, hoping that Tommy would see me and come away from the others, who were all grazing together, and after a while he did. He began to graze his way towards me, and then he broke into a trot and whinnied. Up came Bess's head at the sound of her favourite's voice and she started out in pursuit. There was a broken-down old army hut quite near to me in the field, and I made for it in the hope that I could get Tommy in and mount inside and that the doorway would be too narrow for Bess. But I wasn't quite fast enough. Tommy turned and followed me in his good-natured way, but the furious Bess cut the corner and came charging down on the hut at full gallop. I shot through the doorway just in time, and Bess came to a thundering stop, smacking into the doorway with such force that the old brick building shook and one of the rotting rafters in the roof fell down. It was, thank heavens, too

narrow for her to follow me in; but she blocked it so that
Tommy was kept outside and for more than an hour ram-
paged up and down by the door, snorting and reaching in
with her teeth to grab at me. Once or twice she kicked the
wall of the building. I hoped it hurt.

So there I was, marooned by an angry old half-carthorse.
There was no one to call to for help, and my best plan, I
decided, was to wait until she got bored and started to graze
and then slip on to Tommy's back, where I was fairly sure
I would be safe because she wouldn't risk hurting him. The
difficulty lay in how to get him within range, because Bess
refused to let him come to me when I called but blocked the
way with her body and nipped at him to keep clear.

The minutes I spent in the army hut lengthened into a
very long hour. The building was falling down from lack of
repair, and for all I knew one good shove from Bess could
bring the whole thing down in a heap of rubble; and if that
happened, the nearest bit of cover was a straggly hedge two
hundred yards away. Much too far for me to win a race
against a determined horse.

It settled itself in time. Bess got bored with stamping
around and began to graze, and after a bit the grazing took
her farther away and Tommy came round between her and
the shed. I walked out as quietly as I could and slipped on
to his back. 'Come on, Tom,' I said in his ear. 'For God's sake
get me out of here.' He began to walk towards the gate, Bess
following, and we made a bolt for it in the last few yards
and got through the gate just as Bess came to a jarring stop
on the inside. I stood behind the gate, which was five-barred
and strongly built, watching her. It may be that my memory
is at fault, but I could have sworn that she had yellow eyes.

Chapter 11

RAKE'S PROGRESS

Bess was wanted by the riding school for intensive work for the next six weeks, and so they took her away to live indoors. The man who came down to fetch up the riding school's ponies told me that she was normally a bit nasty in the field, though nothing like as nasty as she had been to me. Probably it was because she was so fond of Tommy, he said, or perhaps I reminded her of her mother-in-law. He went off cackling at his joke, leading Bess, who was docile once caught, from his bicycle. I never saw her again.

Tommy's days, and mine, were busy now. The pony was fit, and thrived on work. Every morning Muffet Hamilton rode him for ten minutes or so, trotting and cantering in circles and figures of eight that would have been difficult for him to manage in a balanced way with my weight on his back. He learned to lead off on the desired leg, taught by cramping his head to the left if he was meant to strike out with the off fore, and by moving the rider's weight back and to the left so that the right shoulder was left free and became the side he would naturally choose to lead with. The aids to lead off to the right – the shortened left rein, the squeeze with both legs, but the firmer squeeze from the left – were given at the same time, so that Tommy learned to lead off as directed without, in the end, any noticeable shift of weight on the rider's part being necessary. Cantering in small circles, though not smaller than twenty yards in diameter, helped a lot in teaching this, as it would have been difficult for Tommy to move on such sharp turns with the outside leg leading. Figure-of-eight canters, coming back to a trot at the crossover point, helped to reinforce what Muffet was trying to teach him, as a different leading leg was required for each circle.

Teaching him to rein back was much easier, and I did this myself. I had often got him to back when I was grooming him and needed more room to get at his face, putting a hand on his nose and saying 'Back' so often that he would almost back from the word alone. On the first few occasions, before he understood what I meant, I had had to push him backwards with a good, firm shove, but once he knew what was wanted, the transition to the more advanced stage of reining back when ridden was easy. Muffet sat on top, collecting him together with a squeeze of the legs while she shortened her reins so that he could feel a light pull on his mouth. It must have seemed to Tommy at first as if he was being asked to go forward and asked to stop both at the same time; but I stood in front of him and put a hand on his nose and said 'Back'. There was really nowhere for him to go in response to all these signals but backwards, so back he went. When he had taken four or five nice straight steps backwards, Muffet loosed the pressure on his reins and made him go forward again, patting him to tell him that he had done well.

There were a couple of things we had to remember about backing. One is that it's no good asking the pony to rein back unless his head is in the right position and his chin flexed, because he'll only get his head up and his balance wrong and make a mess of it. Another is that dragging the pony back by force is hopeless; it hurts his mouth and confuses him, and he isn't likely to back properly if his head is uncomfortable. The third thing is always to loose the rein after several properly executed steps so that the pony goes forward again. A reverse gear on a pony is an asset only as long as the rider has full control of it, and a pony that shoots backwards when someone is trying to hand you a sandwich out hunting is an embarrassment and a pest (and a waster of sandwiches).

The difficulty I have in training ponies, and I have mentioned this before, is in remembering that the pony's perfect obedience to me is not enough. A lovely Anglo-Arab filly I broke in when I was thirteen learned to do a full pass before she was even being ridden at a canter, only because I spent so much time with her that communications between us were excellent. So when, in an idle afternoon, I happened to give her the aids for a full pass – a rather advanced dressage movement – and she did not understand what I meant, I explained it to her by demonstration on the ground, got back on, and was gratified to find that she did it perfectly. She always passaged afterwards when I asked her to, but it must have been from the kindness of her heart rather than from an understanding of the aids because no one else ever got a full pass out of her, and so I had to conclude that I hadn't really taught her anything more than a sort of personal circus trick. A properly trained pony is one who obeys the universal aids used by all riders, and his education is not complete until he will perform for a stranger as readily as he will for his owner. That, weight considerations aside, is why I asked for so much help from Muffet and Louise, and why I was glad to give novice riders like Donald a ride whenever they asked for one.

To return to jumping, the riding school generously lent us the indoor school again, and Louise and I went back with Tommy for a session over higher fences. Louise rode him round once or twice over single cavaletti to remind him what it was all about, and they had a couple of goes over a pair placed thirty inches apart to make him spread. Then I built a pile of three cavaletti about two feet high, and Louise asked him to take the jump properly. He did so happily, allowing her to keep him to a slow canter and then to urge him forward for the last three strides so that they

met the jump at a good place to take off and at a speed which would carry them easily over. This is where having a good schooling rider counts: slowing or increasing the pace shortens or lengthens the pony's stride, and Louise had to judge the final three paces precisely to get Tommy to meet the fence right. They performed very well, though once Tommy took off a full stride too early and only Louise's excellent horsemanship kept her from catching him in the mouth.

I was satisfied with his jumping. He had never refused or run out, either in the school or across country, and only twice had he ever kicked the pole (and that was when he first went scrambling loose around the school with Bimbi). It was tempting to raise the height of the poles to see how much he could manage, and I had to remind myself that he was only three years old and that asking him to do too much could put him off. Anyway, I thought sadly, what's the good of a show jumper who is only 11·2 h.h.?

Afternoons or evenings, whichever time I was free, were spent on cross-country rides (a backing lesson somewhere in each, and sometimes a turn on the forehand) with Bimbi or without; on rides through traffic; on grooming, handling, and a lot of silly behaviour such as jumping on over his backside, crawling about under his feet, flapping dusters and umbrellas at him (he couldn't have cared less). Sometimes on the rides with Bimbi, Grisel led Tommy from her pony while I bawled and clutched and made baby noises and both of us giggled. Neither of the ponies seemed to mind, though I minded very much when one evening we unexpectedly came upon an elderly couple at a turn of the path and the man's, 'Bit old for that, isn't she?' wafted back to us on the evening air.

Chapter 12

THE DARK IS
LIGHT ENOUGH

September came, and with the sadness of the autumn air came the sadness of knowing that the summer of fun with Tommy was coming to an end and that I must look for a home for him where he would be happy and appreciated. His elementary training was complete: he would stand for gates to be opened, had a rudimentary idea of the turn on the forehand, and Muffet had at last persuaded him to do a flying change of legs at a canter. The flying change is as advanced a manoeuvre as the rider of a tiny pony could be expected to know, and Muffet only asked him to do it once or twice because Tommy had had to learn so many things in the past four months that she didn't want to overdo it (wise girl).

He was a pleasure to handle, tolerant of eccentric human behaviour such as vaulting on over his rump, and perfect in traffic. His jumping and cross-country work were very promising, and what he needed now was someone to take him on, school him on, hunt him. I was much too big to take him hunting.

Yet I could not bear the thought of doing without him, and when he came cantering across the field to me in the early autumn evenings, or shoved his little face affectionately up against my body, my throat tightened up and I

sometimes wanted to cry. I put it out of my mind as much as I could, telling myself that the daily reinforcement of his lessons was important for him and that anyway he could not go until we had found a perfect home.

After the hot summer the leaves were changing colour early. Swallows collected on the telephone lines for migration, and at night, as the earth moved once again into the asteroid belt, the sky was full of shooting stars. Wild rose hips started to ripen in the hedgerows. Tommy loved these, and would stand for hours picking them off carefully with his teeth. With the attraction of Bess gone he began again on his wanderings, and one evening at a quarter to eight I got a phone call saying he had been found loose on one of the major roads leading out of Cambridge and had been caught and put into a paddock by some people named Donaldson, whom I had never met. Please would I pick him up?

We happened to have friends staying – fortunately they were people who liked Tommy – and had already dressed to go out to dinner, so I made excuses and ran upstairs and quickly changed into jeans and a jacket. When I came down everyone was waiting for me in the hall, wanting to come on the pony-hunt. We all piled into the car and drove off, not quite sure where we were going. Tommy was approximately where we expected to find him, having a lovely time in a paddock with another pony and a donkey and being looked after by some extremely nice people, who, far from minding about the intruder, seemed to be already rather fond of him.

Night was coming on, and cars on the main road outside the paddock had their headlights on. I could not take Tommy home by the road because we had no lights for him, and an unlit dark-coloured pony on a fast road, apart from being illegal, is very difficult to see. It was shorter to go across country, anyway – only about a mile to his field – but the problem was that I had no idea how well he could see in the dark. I slipped on his headcollar, thanked the kind and friendly Donaldsons, and made a dash for it before the light went completely.

It was much darker than I had expected. There had been some fading light in the open road, but in the shadows of the tall, straggling hedges it was pitch dark, and the newly ploughed soil in the field we were in made us roll and stumble. I vaguely knew that there were streams and hedges in front of us, but I didn't know where they were because I had never been that way before. Anyway, things look different at night. The most worrying thing was the thought of wire: would we be able to see it? I groped down the side of a deep ditch, fell into shallow water, and climbed up the far side through a bank of nettles.

And Tommy jumped as neatly and accurately by my side as if it had been broad daylight. Of course he could see, and of course he knew the way: he had probably strayed over that bit of land lots of times in the past few months. So, as I had done as a child when lost out hunting, I climbed on my pony's back and asked him to take me home. He went over the black land without hesitation, stopping at hedges and ditches for me to dismount and follow him over. Once we met wire, a strand running loosely through an unkempt hedge, but Tommy knew the place where we could duck under it, walking along the hedge until he found it and then standing firmly until his stupid rider understood. There were still the disadvantages of the water, brambles and nettles, which he didn't seem to realize I disliked, but the ride home was fun and I understood why he liked so much to go off by himself.

Too soon we came to the strand of sagging wire at the back end of Tommy's big field, wriggled under it, through a gully and a patch of scrub and on to the path the ponies had worn to the gate. I vaulted on to Tommy's back, and we went like the wind across the field in the night, swerving sometimes with the bend of the path with me hanging on to the mane with both hands. My friends were waiting for us with the car and a bowl of pony nuts for Tommy. 'What kept you so long?' they asked, and I walked into the head-lights scratched and filthy and breathless and they burst out laughing.

Chapter 13

FOR SALE:
CHILD'S PERFECT PONY
WANTED:
PONY'S PERFECT CHILD

I advertised Tommy as 'Child's perfect pony'. It wasn't true in the sense that he was suitable to give elementary lessons, as he was young and enthusiastic and would have got very bored with walking up and down all the time; but it was true in the sense that he was a marvellous companion who would go all day and never tire, and who could be trusted to behave sensibly in all the circumstances I could think of. I hoped he would be bought by someone who liked to hunt (quietly at first, with such a young pony), and jump their way across country, and perhaps school him on a bit. Tommy was, after all, still only three, and the elementary lessons he had learned needed careful reinforcement before he could go on to a more advanced stage at four years old. The most important thing was that he must find an owner who would love him very much, have the sense to ask for expert help if it was needed, and be kind and considerate as well as proud of Tommy. Ponies, like everyone else, need constant care, and you can't leave them without their suppers because it is too nasty to go out or because there's a special programme on television.

How can you put a price on a friend you know so well?

I thought of asking a million pounds for him because there wasn't any sum of money that I would rather have than him, and I thought of giving him away for the same reason. Then I thought of it from the point of view of an unknown buyer, and it seemed to me that unless they were rich enough not to be put off by a fairly high price how would I know that they could afford to feed him properly? So I settled on £85 for my perfect, mongrel, unfashionably coloured three-year-old. And I wrote it down on a piece of paper and worked out that it was his purchase price plus a charge of 7p an hour for training him, and it didn't make sense any way I looked at it.

When the replies to the advertisement came in I read through them abstractedly: these were people who were trying to buy Tommy, and I wasn't looking for a business deal but for a perfect life for him. The temptations for a horse-dealer must be great: for example, one woman called up and asked me if the pony would be suitable for her grandson. She didn't tell me how old the boy was or whether he could ride or what he would do with a pony if he had one, or if he lived in the town or in the country with stabling of his own; just, would Tommy be suitable for her grandson? And for a wild moment I was tempted to reply, 'To be perfectly honest with you, madam, this pony's just what the little gentleman wants. Only I've had so many offers for him that I've had to put the price up to two hundred quid.' Only I didn't, because it was Tommy I was selling and not a piece of furniture. Feeling that the descendant of such an ignorant woman might be a bit short of brains, I told her the pony was too strong and wild for an inexperienced rider, which put her off, as I expect it would most grandmothers.

Finally I got the inquiry I had been hoping for. It came

from a thoroughly nice-sounding Dorset couple called Armstead, who lived in a stretch of forest with their own stabling
and paddocks and had twin eight-year-old daughters who
rode. They already owned an old pony whom they had had
for some time, and the more timid of the girls was quite
happy to go on riding it – but Susan, the more adventurous
twin, wanted a younger and more exciting pony of her own.
Mrs Armstead said that Susan had a natural talent for horses
and thought of nothing else. She also said that they had a
gardener who knew about ponies and would be glad to help
Susan if she needed advice, though Susan would much
rather look after the pony by herself.

W here could you find a better offer? A private home with
its own stabling and grazing and a pony-companion; expert
advice on hand; a forest to run in; a keen young owner who
probably wouldn't grow out of Tommy for three or four
years. And a mother I liked the sound of, who asked me
sensible questions and volunteered the kind of information
I wanted to hear. I said yes please, and that I would bring
the pony down the following week (since if you have to part

with a friend, it is better to do it quickly once your conditions are satisfied).

The last days with Tommy were sad. I tried to behave as if nothing was different, but I ached inside each time he came cantering to my call, each time he followed me into the house, followed loose with his nose to the small of my back, or led the way over a hedge in the country and turned to wait for me with his ears pricked up and a what-fun look about him.

On October 6th I polished him extra-carefully, brushed out his mane and tail until they were smooth and shiny, picked out and polished his feet and gave him an extra big feed for the long journey ahead. It wasn't necessary to tie him up while this was being done; it hadn't been for a long time. When the big cattle truck, which was all I had been able to hire, rattled up to us he didn't start or shy away. The driver let down the back of the truck, and I walked up the ramp into the straw-covered interior and called to Tom to come too. 'Aren't you going to put a halter on it, Miss?' said the driver. No, of course I wasn't.

Tommy came up the ramp, all alone, just as calmly as if he were walking into the kitchen. I told the driver I would like to travel with the pony, and he said just as I liked, but I'd find it a bit cold. It was cold: it was freezing and draughty, and I minded it much more than Tommy, who settled down quite quickly and soon started to eat the hay I had put down for him. After a while the driver stopped and said was I sure I wouldn't be better off riding in the cab? So I climbed in the front with him because I was, after all, only selling a pony. But I felt empty inside.

On the long drive to Dorset we stopped twice, and the driver and I had tea and offered Tommy a drink (didn't want one) and pony nuts (ate those). Six hours after leaving Cambridge we rolled up at a nice house with a couple of paddocks in front of it, and the Armstead family – parents, two boys and twin girls – came out to meet us. The back of the big truck came down, and I led Tommy out on his head-collar. Did Susan Armstead feel as strange as I had felt that afternoon at the end of April when I had watched the unfamiliar little pony walk out of Mr Bray's truck and had known that he was mine?

She went to Tommy and patted him, and her eyes shone. 'Do you think I could have a ride on him?' she asked, as if the pony belonged to me, not to her. I didn't see why not: he looked calm enough, and he would probably be glad to stretch his legs after the long drive. So Susan hopped up on his bare back, picked up the headcollar rope lying on his neck, and was off up the grassy drive at a canter before I had a chance to see whether she knew anything about riding.

She could ride all right. They came cantering back, her plaits flying out behind and Tommy's ears pricked and happy, glad to be out of the boring cattle truck. They rode up and down the drive for a few minutes, and then I weakly asked if I could have a last ride on him and got on and went for a canter on this willing little pony. Somehow we all ended up on the front lawn, where Tommy tucked into the grass and I demonstrated the running vault over his rump to put down a neighbour who had turned up on a hunter and told us that a three-year-old pony was much too wild for a girl of eight. After a while the gardener said hadn't we any sense of responsibility and didn't we know that the pony must be tired after his long journey and ought to have a feed and a bit of quiet? I felt ashamed, as I think we all did, and the gardener led Tommy away to his new stable and Susan and I went too.

The stable was perfect – well-built, thickly bedded down, with fresh water and a small feed for Tommy and good-quality hay. 'Nice little chap,' the gardener said, looking Tommy over thoughtfully, and both Susan and I felt as pleased as if he had paid us a personal compliment.

It was getting late, and the long way home to Cambridge lay ahead. I had been asked back to the house for tea, but Susan would not come too, wanting to stay behind with Tommy. She did not disturb him after his journey, just leaned on the door of the loosebox and watched him while he ate. 'Don't stay too long with him, Susan,' the gardener said to her. 'Give him a chance to settle in.'

So I left them, the young girl and the happy little pony who was just her size. It wasn't easy to go, though I had no doubt at all that Tommy had found himself a perfect home.

Chapter 14

TOMMY REVISITED

I didn't see him again for five years. I think that if you arrange for a pony to start a new life it is fairer to everyone if you do not intrude on it. The Armsteads sent reports that they were pleased with Tommy, and that he was well and happy, and that seemed to be that.

Yet when I came to write about the summer we spent together, and began to relive it in my mind, I badly wanted to have Tommy around again. I called up the Armsteads, afraid that they might have sold the pony since Susan must now be too big for him. But no: they still had Tommy, Mrs Armstead said – they were keeping him for the grand-children (which I took to mean for ever, as Susan was only thirteen and the other children not much older). They had four other ponies, all bigger, so there were plenty to ride and I was welcome to borrow Tommy for a few weeks if it would help with the book.

I hired a horsebox and drove down to Dorset to fetch him. The Armsteads had moved to a new house in a wild part of the forest, and to get to it you had to go down almost a mile of gravelled track and then across a twenty-acre field. There were three ponies in the field, all of them curious for a close look at the horsebox, but none of them was Tommy. Susan cantered up bareback on a lovely part-bred Arab stallion whom she was breaking in and told me that Tommy was probably in the garden, if he hadn't let himself out.

It sounded as if Tommy was not much changed. Mr Armstead confirmed it: he said that the twenty-acre field had originally been four paddocks, but that they had taken down the dividing fences because Tommy got through them so easily that they might just as well not have been there. The current problem was keeping Tommy in the big field, at which they were largely unsuccessful. It would be all right, Mr Armstead said, trying to sound annoyed but not doing very well, if it was only Tommy who wandered when he felt like it, but he almost always let his gang out with him. Though the Armsteads obviously thought this funny, neighbours with trampled gardens did not always share the joke.

We went out into the Armsteads' garden, which (I apologize to them) was a bit of a ruin, too. On what had been planned as a neat stretch of lawn a small, fat pony grazed, tearing up mouthfuls of newly planted grass by the roots. He had a long, thick mane, a magnificent tail which swept the ground, and the width of his stomach and shoulders would have done credit to a prize bull. None the less, he was obviously Tommy.

I took him home with me. He was the Tommy I remembered – affectionate, willing, enthusiastic, though his body had grown so strong that I easily believed the Armsteads' claim that he would stay all day out hunting, and his manners were much improved by Susan's work with him. Good manners notwithstanding, in the two short months that he stayed with me he got up to the following tricks:

He ran away with me twice (I was riding him bareback in a halter and had thought my weight would be enough to hold him, but I hadn't reckoned with the adult strength of Tommy) ...

He broke the rope that tethered him in my garden (my fault for using him to cut the grass) and disappeared towards my landlord's farm. I heard him clatter past my bedroom – I was changing for a hunt – and followed as soon as I was dressed. The landlord's wife met me outside her house.

'Have you lost something?' she asked, looking curiously at my formal black jacket and bowler.

'Yes,' I said. 'I'm looking for my hunter.'

'Try our vegetable garden,' said my landlord's wife. I found him in the brussels sprouts ...

We kept him on the farm in a paddock fenced with three-rail wooden post-and-rails. He had two other ponies in the paddock with him, and I thought that with such stout fencing and good company he was secure. Not so: he didn't especially like the ponies he was pastured with, but over the fence was a horse who really took his eye – an 18·2 h.h. thoroughbred chestnut event horse. Tommy kicked out the middle rail in one section of the fencing and jumped through the gap to be with his new love; I put him back in his own paddock, tied up the broken fence with string and hoped he wouldn't notice how weak my repair job was. I shall never know whether he did or not, whether it was contempt for my feeble mending or a general statement that trying to keep him in was pointless, but the following morning there were *seven* broken rails in the paddock fence, bottom, top, and middle rails arbitrarily along the line, and Tommy and both the other ponies were in with the chestnut eventer. Maybe it was Tommy's idea of a joke. Anyway, all of us laughed, even the owner of the fence ...

The chestnut eventer, who was so big that Tommy could

walk under his stomach, ate some of his little friend's mane and all of his forelock.

When I took Tommy home again to Dorset, the first thing Susan Armstead said was, 'I don't think much of his haircut.' Tommy's pony gang clustered around the horsebox, and Tommy, eager to be out with them, started to kick his way free. We hurriedly let down the back of the box and Tommy came out in a swirl of shiny brown fur. The others pushed up close to smell him and say hello, and a curious, graceful pony ballet took place, circling, rearing, dancing ponies, pleased to see each other after two months' absence. They wheeled together in a wild charge of delight, thundering over the turf, bucking, turning, swooping back. By the time they had settled the early winter light had begun to fade and it was no longer easy to see which one was Tommy. Susan went out, calling to him, and he came to her out of the gathering dark. They stood with their heads not quite touching, in a long, glad silence while the night came in and covered them.